BODY LANGUAGE AND DARK PSYCHOLOGY:

THE COMPLETE GUIDE TO SPEED-READING, ANALYZE PEOPLE AND MASTER THE SECRETS OF HUMAN BEHAVIOR WITH MANIPULATION AND MIND CONTROL

Navarro Goleman & Joe Poumpouras

TABLE OF CONTENTS

INTRODUCTION 5

CHAPTER 1-   WHAT IS NON-VERBAL COMMUNICATION 10

CHAPTER 2-   PERSONALITY TYPES 21

CHAPTER 3-   FEET AND LEGS 29

CHAPTER 4-   TORSO 35

BODY POSTURE 35
TORSO 43

CHAPTER 5-   ARMS 45

ARMS, HANDS AND FINGERS...45
EMPHATIC GESTURES 51
SUGGESTIVE GESTURES..52
PROMPTING GESTURES..54

CHAPTER 6-   FACE 58

FACIAL EXPRESSIONS 58
IMPORTANCE OF EYES...59
MICRO EXPRESSIONS 61
THE INFLUENCE OF SMILES 64
HEAD MOVEMENTS 66

CHAPTER 7-   VOICE 69

TONE 69
THE SPEED OF A SPEECH 71

CHAPTER 8-   UNIVERSAL NON-VERBAL SIGNS..................... 73

CHAPTER 9-   HOW TO SPOT LIE... 81

THE BEHAVIORAL DELAY OR PAUSE 82
THE VERBAL OR NON-VERBAL DISCONNECT 84
HIDING THE EYES OR THE MOUTH...85
SWALLOWING OR THROAT CLEARING 86

THE HAND-TO-FACE ACTIONS 87
THE NOSE TOUCH 88
EYE RUB.. 90

CHAPTER 10-   SPOTTING ROMANTIC INTEREST 91

CHAPTER 11-   TIPS 102

TIPS ON HOW TO IMPROVE YOUR NON-VERBAL COMMUNICATION... 102
TIPS ON HOW TO PROTECT YOURSELF FROM DECEPTION 108

CHAPTER 12-   DECEPTION 113

TYPES OF DECEPTION... 114
MOTIVES FOR DECEPTION.. 116
DECEPTION TECHNIQUES 116

CHAPTER 13-   BODY LANGUAGE OF ATTRACTION...........120

THE ATTRACTION SIGNALS 121
TOUCH... 124

CHAPTER 14-   MIRRORING..128

WHAT IS MIRRORING?... 129
USES OF MIRRORING 131
HOW TO MIRROR 132

CHAPTER 15-   BODY LANGUAGE APPLICATIONS 137

**CHAPTER 16-   BEHAVIOR,   DEVIANT   BEHAVIOR   AND
PSYCHOLOGY   149**

DEVIANT BEHAVIOR AND PSYCHOLOGY 152
PSYCHOLOGY OF ADDICTIVE BEHAVIOR 155
WHAT DOES MALE BEHAVIOR TELL US 160
PSYCHOLOGY OF WOMEN... 161

**CHAPTER 17-   INTERPRETING   AND   UNDERSTANDING
PERSONALITY TYPE AND THEIR MAIN CHARACTERISTICS 163**

CONCLUSION 177

Introduction

What Is Body Language?

Body language is a notion, which men and women that are effective often know well. The analysis and concept of it are become popular lately years since we can comprehend exactly what we 'state' during our bodily gestures and facial expressions, to interpret and show our inherent feelings and perspectives. Body language can also be known as 'non-verbal communications', and much less generally 'on-vocal communications. The term 'same-sex' will be utilized at a wider awareness, and each of these conditions is somewhat obscure. For this guide, the terms 'body language' and 'non-verbal communications' are widely interchangeable. This manual also has the view it is the analysis of how people communicate facial besides the spoken words, and in this regard, the treatment of this topic here is wider than normal guides, that are restricted only to human gestures and positions.

If you execute any serious analysis or debate, you should explain the language on your way.

As an instance:

Body language that is does comprise attention and facial expression movement. – Normally, what about perspiration and breathing? - This is dependent upon the definition used. And while pitch and tone of voice signs; is such part of body language? Not normally, but so if considering bodily gestures/expressions and just the phrases, because they could ignore by you. There are no replies to those questions. It is an issue of interpretation. For broadening our range, a reason is to avoid missing important signals which may not be contemplated inside a narrower definition. Nevertheless, confusion arises if definitions and context aren't correctly created, for instance: It's carelessly and commonly quoted that 'on-verbal communications' or 'body language' accounts for as many as 93 percent of their significance that individuals take from any individual communication. This is a simulation-based on the study concept, which while it is something of a basis of body language study didn't create such a claim of Albert Mehrabian. Mehrabian's research findings centered on communications with a strong psychological or 'feelings' component besides, the 93% non-verbal percentage included vocal intonation (paralinguistic), which can be considered by most as falling out the definition. When saying specific care must be resolved figures concerning proportions of conveyed, or in making any company claims concerning communications and body language. It's safe to state that body language signifies a very large percentage of meaning that is conveyed and translated between individuals. Resources and body language specialists appear to agree that between 50-80percent of communications are non-invasive. So, while the data change based on the circumstance, it's usually accepted that non-invasive communications are extremely important in the way we know each other (or fail to), particularly in face-to-face and one-way communications, and most certainly when the communications demand a psychological or sociological element. When we meet somebody for body language is particularly crucial the very first moment. We create and this evaluation relies far more on what we believe in and see about another person that they speak. We produce an opinion about an individual that is brand new before they speak a word. This is quite powerful in forming impressions on meeting somebody. The result occurs both ways - from when we meet with somebody for the very first-time language, the unconscious and conscious levels determine our perception of them.

When someone meets with us, they form their impression from our signs most of us. And this influence continues throughout communications and relationships between individuals. Body language translated and is continually being exchanged on a subconscious level this is occurring Involving individuals of this time. Remember - while you're interpreting (consciously or unconsciously) yours is being continuously interpreted by the body language of individuals, so men and women. The individuals and, with the awareness of abilities body language often get an edge over those whose admiration is restricted to the subconscious.

You may change your consciousness from the unconscious mindful by studying the topic, and then by practicing, you're studying communications on your dealings with other people.

Chapter 1 What is Non-verbal Communication

Have you heard of the phrase "it's not what you say it's how you say it"? There is true meaning behind this as, what we say matters, sure, but the non-verbal cues we give are even more important.. It has been said that more than sixty percent of what you say is in your body language not your actual words.

Learning about non-verbal communication can help you in a variety of ways. You will be more perceptive to what people are actually trying to say. You may also pick up on lies or deceit more easily. Figuring out a person's true motivation can become much clearer when you start to pay attention to what their body is saying.

Paralanguage is part of non-verbal communication. It encompasses a couple of different areas that can help you communicate more effectively. The main pieces of it are tone, cadence, and inflection. All of these elements play a key role in what you are actually saying.

The tone of your voice plays a pretty big role in non-verbal communication, as well. It can draw a listener in or make them totally tune out. A voice that is monotone does not have any inflection. Every word comes out with the same tone and volume. The cadence of a monotone speaker tends to be slow and steady throughout their words. This can be very hard to listen too.

When you are talking with someone changing your tone can help to give them clues as to how you are feeling. It allows for better communication as we are able to express our emotions through the tone of our voices. In public speaking, having a great tone will get you everywhere. Voice inflection is just as important, and both play a big role in effective verbal communication.

If you have a flat voice or you notice that people drift off while you are talking you can practice this. Find your favorite book and practice reading it aloud with different inflections and tones. This can help you during regular conversations to get away from the monotone nature of some voices. You will notice that people around you are more engaged and what you say matters more than it did before.

Para communication is only a piece of non-verbal communication. What else do we need to consider when trying being better non-verbal communicators. This is a tough question as there is quite a bit that encompasses non-verbal communication. We can take a bit of time and look at the tip of the iceberg but know that people spend years studying non-verbal communication.

Reading someone's facial expressions is a major tell in non-verbal communication. There are many exercises that teach us what facial expressions are saying. Some of them are very straightforward. If you look at someone that is smiling it, typically, means they are happy or enjoying what they are doing. However, a smile can be deceiving.

Smiling can also be a sign of anxiety. When people want to fit in but don't know how to do that, they will smile to look more approachable and less nervous. Tight lips can give away these smiles. You may also notice that a smile on someone's face simply looks fake. If you feel this way, it likely is. That goes along with going with your gut.

The more you notice about someone's expression the more you can tell about them. Sure, picking out a smile or a frown is easy but what about the smaller harder to see expressions. Our faces have up to ten thousand different movement patterns and believe it or not they all mean something. Learning more about what facial twitches and twists mean can help you pick out the rats among the group.

Kinesics, or body movement, also play a major role in non-verbal communication, the gestures that we make during conversations tell a lot about how we are feeling. If we are interested in what is being said or we are nervous about it. Paying attention to how people's bodies are moving will tell you volumes about what they are thinking and feeling.

Think about the last meeting you were sitting in, did you see the person nervously drumming their fingers on the table or their thighs? This is a sign of boredom, irritability, and nervousness. This can be very distracting to a group and should be avoided. If you are one to take to these body movements keep in mind that the best thing you can do is keep your hands on the table. Clasping them can help keep you from the annoying drumming that your feelings are pushing you toward.

We are used to the meaning of some body movements. When we are having a conversation and someone is looking at us and nodding as we speak, we know this means they are paying attention and actively listening to what we have today. Some may be nodding but not actually engaged. You can see this through their eye movement. This could be from boredom or preoccupied thinking.

While both of these examples are easy to spot there are a few body movements that aren't as easy to determine meaning from. Someone that frequently clears their throat is likely nervous about what they are saying, however, they may just be trying to get someone's attention that is distracted.

Nervous ticks are commonly seen in people that are going to do something against the law or something harmful to others. Unless you are deep in the traits of the Dark Triad, you likely feel some sort of guilt when doing something wrong. This can lead to body movement clues as your body is rejecting the act that is about to be performed.

Noticing these ticks can give you great insight as to the intentions of a person. It can be a simple twitch of the hand or odd mouth movements. It could even be a jerking of the head or other limbs. So, while bouncing of knees or drumming of fingers are consistent views that somebody is nervous or bored. There are tells when somebody has something worse on their mind.

Another major component in non-verbal communication is eye contact. It can be very difficult for some people to maintain eye contact. This can make you feel as if they are not listening or that they are

Shifty. For some, it is neither of these things. They simply find it to be uncomfortable to look somebody in the eyes while talking.

Maintaining a certain level of eye contact with somebody you are talking to shows that you are interested and engaged in what they are saying. This does not mean that you need to stare at them the entire time that they are talking. However, frequent eye contact can truly help improve communication.

Experts have found that when looking somebody in the eye it can be more comfortable when you look at their other features as well. Varying your site to look at their eyelids nose and around the other areas of their face can make it less uncomfortable. Of course, you will also want to take the time to actually look them in the eyes as they are speaking.

People that have committed crimes or that intend on committing crimes have a hard time maintaining contact. It has been said that the eyes are the window to the soul and there is definitely some truth in this. When you notice how somebody's eyes move and look it can help you to determine their intent whether it be good or bad.

When looking at nonverbal communication and people that truly command attention a lot of it is said through their posture. Your posture says a lot about not only you and your confidence levels but also your position in life. When we talked about your posture we're not only speaking of when you're standing up at also plays a role when you are sitting down.

Open and closed posture also play a role in how people perceive you. If you are accepting of people coming up and talking to you, you will want to use an open posture. This looks like a pretty relaxed position. Your shoulders and hips will be equally spread and you won't be standing at attention. You will leave your stomach exposed rather than crossing your arms over top of it. Standing this way makes you more approachable. It will make it so that people trust you more easily and are willing to have conversations with you at any point.

A closed pasture going to have the exact opposite effect, if you were sitting in the chair with your arms crossed over your stomach and your legs crossed, as well, you are telling people to stay away. This type of positioning can make it look like you are very bored. It also tells people that you are unapproachable and unwilling to open up to them. This causes distrust and tends to lead to poor communication.

Proxemics is another important factor in nonverbal communication. This genuinely has to do with people's personal space and their comfort levels. Most people want you to stay outside of their "personal bubble". Most are comfortable standing in conversation with somebody they don't know when that person is a foot or more away from them. Obviously, the people that we care about can be closer to us without making us uncomfortable. This goes for family members, people you are in relationships with, and close friends.

Taking notice to not only other people's personal space but your own is important. Some people that would like to victimize you will try and get in close. They realize that touching somebody makes a connection. They will

Honan on their ability to come into close contact with you and then take advantage of it. So making sure that you stand a reasonable distance away from people will stop this behavior from occurring. In addition, if somebody is a bit touchy feely there is nothing wrong with telling them that it makes you uncomfortable. Letting them know that it is not okay to be in your personal space can save you from harm in the future.

In a business atmosphere, you want to make sure that you are not overly far away from someone. If you are very far away during a conversation and it may seem as if you are disinterested. It is easier to get distracted while somebody is talking if you're not near to them. Knowing the appropriate distance four conversations is important for most people. It's really can help you to communicate more effectively.

The last area to look at and nonverbal communication is psychological changes. These can be quite hard to notice but with practice it can become easier. This type of communication is related to our emotions. When we use the word psychological changes, we are talking about noticing if somebody starts to sweat or their face turns red from embarrassment. These are surefire ways to tell that somebody is feeling uncomfortable or uneasy about their current situation.

If you are dealing with a friend that gets teary-eyed while you're talking you probably need to change your tactics to make them feel more comfortable. Putting somebody at ease when they are feeling nervous can truly help to build your rapport with them. Of course, you want to be careful when dealing with people that you don't know very well. They can pick up on your psychological changes and, in turn, use them against you.

Chapter 2 Personality Types

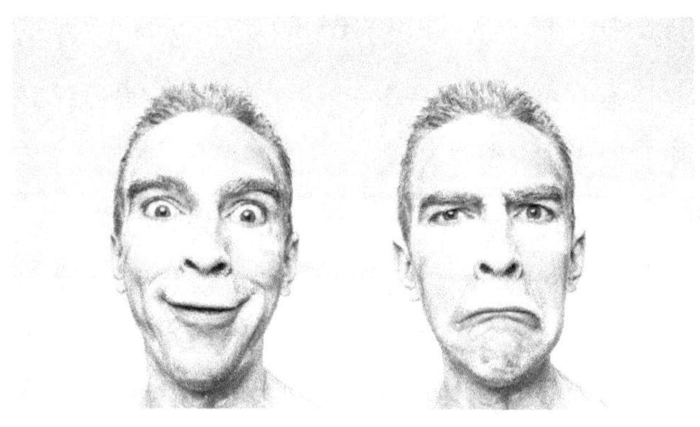

W hen you interact with a person for a while, you can interpret and tell the type of personality they are. Personality type refers to the different types of individuals as have been classified through psychology based on the way they tend to behave, feel, and think. Personality is what makes a person who they are, and each person has an idea of their personality type. Some people are thick-skinned, others are sensitive, and others are bubbly while others are reserved.

Several ways have been put forward to measure personality, but mostly, psychologists focus on personality traits. The Big Five has come to be the most widely accepted of these traits. It is also called the FFM standing for the five-factor model or the OCEAN.

These five factors are the ones expressed by the acronym CANOE or OCEAN. These factors are affected by how someone was brought up. Genetics and the environment affect these personality traits almost equally. Let us dive in and analyze each of these five broad types of personalities and the attributes associated with each one of them so that you can know to interpret them.

Extraversion

This is the widely recognized personality type. It is common for you to hear people say that someone is either an extrovert or an introvert. This personality type is based on someone having a lot of interaction with the external world. Extraverts are known to be a kind of social butterflies and drive pleasure from interactions with others and are often known to be full of energy.

They are lively, sociable, and chatty, and they draw power and energy from their interactions with crowds. They are action-oriented persons and tend to be enthusiastic. They are assertive and talkative and have high group visibility .they may dominance in social settings.

On the other hand, introverts have lower energy and are less involved with the social world. They have lower engagement with the social world and deliberately tend to be low-key and quiet. This should not be confused with being shy or depressed but being more independent of their social world. Being shy refers to the fear of social situations and interactions or being unable to function socially, but an introvert can be charming at parties and come-together events with colleagues. They like to have their time alone and require less social stimulation, not because they are antisocial or unfriendly, but because they are reserved in social events. They just prefer being solo or in small-group activities.

Agreeableness

Individuals with this personality have a general concern for social harmony. People with agreeable personality place premium value in getting along well with others, and they have the willingness to consider other people even if it means sacrificing self-interests. They are associated with kindness, being helpful, generosity, and being trusting and trustworthy. They are optimistic about their look of humanity.

On the other hand, disagreeable individuals put their self-interest first at the expense of good relations with others. They have less concern about other peoples' wellbeing and will rarely reach out for others. They tend not to be friendly or cooperative because they are skeptical and suspicious of others. They are seen as being argumentative, challenging, competitive, or untrustworthy people.

Openness

People with this type of personality are open to the experience. They have a general appreciation for adventure, art, imagination, unusual ideas, emotion, and other experiences. They are open to the excitement, have intellectual curiosity, sensitive to beauty, and are always ready to experiment with new things. They have a good understanding of their feelings and are associated with creativity. Scoring high on openness may be taken to mean that they are hard to predict, can hold unconventional beliefs, may lack focus, and indulge in risky behavior such as taking drugs. Individuals in this category seek to actualize themselves through euphoric and intense experiences.

Conversely, people with low openness are pragmatic and data-driven and seek to gain fulfillment through endurance. They are seen to have closed minds and are perceived to be dogmatic. They are better off sticking to their habits, avoid adventurous activities, and tend not to like new experiences.

Neuroticism

Individuals in this category tend to experience negative emotions. These emotions include depression, anger, or anxiety. It is associated with emotional instability and connected to low tolerance for stress or aversive stimuli. Scoring high in neuroticism scales means that the individual is emotionally reactive and susceptible to stress. They tend towards being loose and disrespectful in the way they express their emotions. They make a mountain out of small issues. More likely, they may misinterpret an ordinary situation and see it as a threat. It becomes hopelessly tricky for them when they encounter minor frustrations.

Neuroticism is interlinked with a defeatist attitude and being pessimistic towards work, apparent anxiety towards work, and the confidence that work hinders personal relationships. Scoring high in neuroticism is connected with a high possibility to show skin-conductance reactivity, with diminished ability to regulate emotions which affects one's capability to think with clarity, make sound choices and deal with stress effectively. People who score high in neuroticism lack contentment with their achievements in life and have a high chance of falling into clinical depression. They tent to go through more negative life events; their psychological wellbeing is worse off.

On the other hand, those scoring less on neuroticism are hardly annoyed and have less emotional reactivity. They are usually calm and have emotional stability. They do not experience persistent negative feelings.

Conscientiousness

This personality type is marked with the ability to show self-discipline. Individuals in this category have a strong sense of duty and strive to achieve without paying much attention to external expectations or measures. They are excellent planners, focused on achievement, dependable, and disciplined. They understand how to regulate, control, and give direction to their impulses. Stubbornness and focus are associated with high conscientiousness.

Low conscientiousness is perceived as being flexible, freewheeling, and spontaneous, but sometimes it can appear as a lack of reliability and sloppiness and may tend to be careless. It is a helpful personality trait and has been connected to better achievement in school and the workplace.

With such knowledge, you can interact with a person for a while, interpret, and tell the type of personality they have.

28

Chapter 3 Feet and Legs

When engaging in a conversation, we typically don't pay attention to the movements of the lower body. Since our direct line of sight is from the chest up, we often miss the obvious signs of the legs and feet. Certain stances that occur within the legs can signify dominance, sexual attraction, and even anxiety. Let's consider a few common patterns to look for when attempting to analyze someone else.

Crossed Legs

Crossed legs could indicate defensiveness. Perhaps you are sitting in a meeting at work, and your colleague says something totally off-putting. You may find yourself slowly crossing your legs as a subliminal way of showing your disapproval. Defensiveness could be heightened when one hand is positioned on top of the crossed leg. This is almost like a taunting move, signaling combat.

Crossing the ankles or knees are signs of nervousness, anxiety, and fear. This stance is protective in nature, which indicates that someone is attempting to protect themselves from whatever source of fear they are encountering. It could also be a means to control actions during high adrenaline situations.

Pointing and Active Legs

If you are miserable at a party, likely your legs are pointed towards the door as you are ready to leave. Our legs inadvertently point to where our heart wants to go. This can be used to determine interest and attraction. The legs, even when covered, will almost always point in the direction they are interested in.

Legs that bounce continuously could mean two things: boredom and nervousness. When you witness a person continuously bouncing their legs up and down, they may be nervous about something. This bounce is like a protective blanket that distracts their mind from their jitters. In addition, when someone is growing restless and ready to go, they may move their legs rapidly. The bouncing or tapping of the legs can be likened to a compulsion carried out to make the irritation subside.

When both legs point in one direction, it could be a clear indicator of interest for the person. However, when one leg steps back, it could indicate that the person wants distance. They may be uncomfortable with the person, conversation, or situation at hand. This subtle movement could be their way of escaping something distressful.

Messages from the Thighs

The upper portions of the legs usually indicate sexual or suggestive invitations between men and women. In daily activities, men may sit with their thighs opened as a sign of dominance. This outward display of masculinity represents an "alpha male" mentality. With women, closed thighs are a polite sign of femininity. Many young girls are instructed to sit with their legs closed so as not to expose their private areas. This closed manner of sitting is graceful and emanates class. When opened, they express dominance and even a form of female rebellion. Since it is so common for girls to be taught to keep their legs closed, doing the opposite could indicate opposition to societal norms. In addition, it is also extremely flirtatious to sit with the thighs crossed and one sitting higher above the other. This could indicate interest.

The Feet

The feet work very closely with the legs to determine areas of interest. When the toes are pointed at a specific object or direction, this indicates where we want to go. This could be a subtle signal your body sends to your mind about certain situations. The feet are used to make a statement and could also be used as an accent to verbal cues. Stomping, imaginative kicking, or tapping are all means of gaining attention.

When toddlers throw tantrums, it's not only their flailing arms, crying eyes, and yelling demands that occur. Toddlers utilize their legs and feet to create loud noises to further emphasize their anger.

Much like moving the legs, bouncing the feet or excessive pacing are signs of anxiety. During moments of high adrenaline, the feet can be seen moving uncontrollably, almost like rabbit's feet. Signs of nervousness are also present when the feet are curled behind an object, perhaps the legs of a chair or a table. Since curving the body inward is a subtle sign of inner protection, the feet follow suit with this protective stance.

Professor Geoffrey Beattie of the University of Manchester reveals that subtle foot movements and positioning could reveal signs of personality traits. He explains, "The weird thing about feet is that most people know what they are doing with their facial expressions; they may or may not know what they are doing with their hands, but unless we specifically think about it, we know nothing about what we are doing with our feet." Through his studies, he found that individuals with rather arrogant or haughty personalities typically kept their feet still as they were always aware of the self; whereas, shy individuals frequently shuffled their feet when sitting. This gives us insight into the characteristics of a person. Typically, shy people indicate high levels of nervousness or anxiety during social occasions. This directly proves the notion that foot movement equals anxiety. The beauty behind interpreting subtle body movements is that you can always find a glimmer of proof to solidify the theory.

Feet are also directly related to laughter. When we are extremely tickled by something, our feet come slightly off the ground. We may even partner that laughter with a slap of the knee. Dr. Beattie mentioned that men and women subconsciously show their attraction by combining feet movement during laughter. This indicates that the woman is comfortable enough with you to make obvious movements. As far as men, he says, "With men, feet aren't so important.

When it comes to interpreting the signs of the legs and feet, direction and movement are the two primary components needed for translation. Although we typically fret from glancing at the bottom half of a person, simple movements could be a key indicator as to how a person is feeling. It's imperative to understand the beauty of intricate movements in order to fully understand the inner workings of another person.

Chapter 4 Torso

Body Posture

Expectedly, posture, and body orientation should be interpreted in the context of the entire body language to develop the full meaning being communicated. Starting with an open posture, it is used to denote amicability and positiveness.

In this open position, the feet are placed openly, and the palms of the hands are facing outward. Individuals with open posture are deemed more persuasive compared to those with other stances.

To realize an open stance, one should stand upright or sit straight with the head upright and maintain the abdomen and chest bared. When the open posture is combined with an easy facial expression and good visual contact, it makes one look approachable and composed. Maintain the body facing forward toward the other person during a conversation.

There is also the closed posture where one crosses the arms across the chest or crosses the legs or sits in a facing a forward position as well as displaying the backs of the hands and closing the fists are indicative of a closed stance.

The closed posture gives the impression that one is bored, hostile, or detached. In this posture, one is acting cautious and appears ready to defend themselves against any accusation or threat.

For the confident posture, it helps communicate that one is not feeling anxious, nervous, or stressed. The confident posture is attained by pulling oneself to full height, holding the head high, and keeping the gaze at eye level. Then bring your shoulders backward and keep the arms as well as legs to relax by the sides. The posture is likely to be used by speakers in a formal context such as when making a presentation, during cross-examination and during project presentation.

Equally important, there is postural echoing and is used as a flirting technique by attracting someone in the Guardian. It is attained by observing and mimicking the style of the person and the pace of movement. When the individual leans against the wall, replicate the same.

By adjusting your postures against the others to attain a match, you are communicating that you are trying to flirt with the individual. The postural echoing can also be used as a prank game to someone you are familiar with and often engage in casual talk.

Maintaining a straight posture communicates confidence and formality. Part of the confidence of this posture is that it maximizes blood flow and exerts less pressure on the muscle and joints, which enhances the composure of an individual. The straight posture helps evoke desirable mood and emotion, which makes an individual feel energized and alert. A straight posture is highly preferred informal conversations such as during meetings, presentation, or when giving a speech.

Correspondingly being in a slumped position and hunched back is a poor posture and makes one be seen as lazy, sad, or poor. A slumped position implies a strain to the body, which makes the individual feel less alert and casual about the ongoing conversation.

On the other hand, leaning forward and maintaining eye contact suggests that one is listening keenly. During a speech, if the audience leans forward in an upright position, then it indicates that they are eager and receptive to the message.

Furthermore, if one slants one of the shoulders when participating in a conversation, then it suggests that the individual is tired or unwell. Leaning on one side acutely while standing or sitting indicates that you are feeling exhausted or fed up with the conversation and are eagerly waiting for the end or for a break.

Think of how you or others reacted when a class dragged on to almost break time. There is a high likelihood that the audience slanted one of their shoulders to left or right direction. In this state, the mind of the individual deviates to things that one will do next. In case of a tea break, the mind of the students will deviate to what one will do during or after the tea break.

By the same measure standing on one foot indicates that one is feeling unease or tired. When one stands on one foot, then it suggests that the person is trying to cope with uncomforting. The source of uneasiness could be emotional or physiological.

For instance, you probably juggled your body from one foot to help ease the need to go for a short call or pass wind. It is a way to disrupt the sustained concentration that may enhance the disturbing feeling.

If one cups their head or face with their hands and rests the head on the thighs, then the individual is feeling ashamed or exhausted.

When the speaker mentions something that makes you feel embarrassed, then one is likely to cup their face or head and rest the face on the thighs. It is a literal way of hiding from shame.

Children are likely to manifest this posture though while standing. When standing this posture may make one look like he or she is praying.

Additionally, if one holds their arms akimbo while standing, then the individual is showing a negative attitude or disapproval of the message. The posture is created by holding the waist with both hands while standing up straight and facing the target person. The hands should simultaneously grip on the flanks, the part near the kidneys. In most cases, the arms-akimbo posture is accompanied by disapproval or sarcastic face to denote attitude, disdain, or disapproval.

When one stretches both of their shoulders and arms and rests them on chairs on either side, then the individual is feeling tired and casual. The posture is akin to a static flap of wings where one stretches their shoulder and arms like wings and rests them on chairs on either side. It is one of the postures that loudly communicates that you are bored, feeling casual, and that you are not about the consequences of your action.

The posture is also invasive of the privacy and space of other individuals and may disrupt their concentration.

If one bends while touching both of their knees, then the individual is feeling exhausted and less formal with the audience. The posture may also indicate extreme exhaustion and need to rest.

For instance, most soccer players bend without kneeling while holding both of their knees, indicating exhaustion. Since in this posture, one is facing down, the posture may be highly inappropriate in formal contexts and may make one appear queer.

When one leans their head and supports it with an open palm on the cheeks, then it indicates that one is thinking deep and probably feeling sad, sorrowful or depressed.

The posture is also used when one is watching something with a high probability of negative outcomes such as a movie or a game. The posture helps one focus deep on the issue akin to meditating.

Through this posture, an individual try to avoid distractions and think deeper on what is being presented.

If you watch European soccer, you will realize that coaches use this posture when trying to study the match, especially where their team is down. However, this posture should not be used in formal contexts as it suggests rudeness. The posture should be used among peers only.

Then there is the crossing of the legs from the thigh through the knee while seated on a chair, especially on a reclining chair. In this posture, one is communicating that he or she is feeling relaxed and less formal.

In most cases, this posture is exhibited when one is at home watching a movie or in the office alone past working hours. If this posture is replicated in a formal context, then it suggests boredom or lack of concentration.

For the posture where one crosses the legs from the ankle to the soles of the feet while seated, it communicates that one is trying to focus in an informal context such as at home. For instance, if a wife or a child asks the father about something that he has to think through, then the individual is likely to exhibit this posture. If this posture is replicated in a formal context, then it suggests boredom or lack of concentration.

Torso

As the legs take up quite a portion of the body, they can also force the torso to lean certain ways. This is an added means of reading the nonverbal messages that the legs are giving out.

Our torso is a substantial body part that we communicate through. When you think of body language, you probably think of somebody's face, how they use their arms, or maybe the way that they use their legs.

The torso has specific signals that matter as well. Within your chest are the rest of the critical parts of your body. While your head is like the control center, it's pointless if everything else doesn't work. You could lose an arm or a leg and still be perfectly able to survive. You would not be able to drop your stomach or your heart, because you wouldn't be able to function, you could get a transplant, of course, but our bodies cannot live without these things. This means that this is a part of our body that we are going to protect the most.

Your brain is going to focus on making sure that if you feel uncomfortable. As mentioned before, you might cross your arms as a way to protect your torso.

We have to remember that this is going to show through our body language more than most subconscious movements. You're making certain moves to try and protect this part of your body. For example, somebody might curl up in the fetal position with their arms over their chests. This is because they're trying to comfort themselves and feel a little bit more protected.

Chapter 5 Arms

Arms, Hands and Fingers

Your hands are the gateway to communicating your feelings to the world. People tend to focus more on the slightest movement of the hands and fingers as compared to the rest of the body. Why? It boils down to evolution once again. As humans evolved and moved to an upright position, the hands have become more expressive, skilled, and also more dangerous.

Therefore, we tend to focus more on the hand movements to gauge what people are saying and to see if they have bad intentions. People find those with expressive use of hand movement as persuasive and of high credibility.

The Appearance of the Hand Speaks Volumes

It is relatively easy to assess a person's line of work by looking at their hands. The hands of an individual who spends all day typing on a system will often have a dainty and slender look. On the other hand, laborer's hand will have a certain rough and calloused appearance.

A pianist or guitarist is likely to have calluses on the fingers. Athletes are likely to have more scars than most people.

The way people take care of their hands is also an important factor to consider when dealing with people. An individual with perfectly manicured long nails is perceived as someone who values social conventions. Nail-biting is often seen as a sign of nervousness or insecurity.

Analyze People through Their Handshakes

Have you ever shaken hands with someone, and it felt as if your hand was being crushed? Perhaps you've been put off by a weak and "limpy" handshake before? Some people don't realize that the power to make a good impression resides in their hands since it's often the first point of physical contact with another person.

The handshake is a defining moment in your relationship with another. It will give you a first-hand feel of the person you are dealing with.

Certain people have decided to turn a simple handshake into an opportunity to assert dominance, which can be annoying since it is an intentional ploy to subdue the other party. Some go a little further by employing the "politician's handshake," which involves using the left hand to cover a handshake. These types of handshakes tend to alienate rather than make a good impression.

Take Note of Cultural Differences

In the Middle East, for instance, it is a sign of respect when two men hold hands together for long periods. You are likely to meet uncomfortable stares if you attempt this in Western cultures.

If you are planning to travel to new places, try to understand the culture and norms of your destination. If someone from the Middle East region and some parts of Asia wants to hold your hand, let them! Don't be surprised if your Russian male host kisses you on the cheek. Don't rebuff these gestures since it warms people up to you and makes them easier to analyze.

Analyzing Nonverbals of the Arms

Up to now, we have examined the importance of appearance and the way our hand movements dictate our credibility. Now let's examine nonverbals of the arms that will help us know what others are feeling and thinking.

Offensive Hand Displays

Finger Pointing

In many countries, finger pointing is seen as a very offensive and distasteful hand gesture. It is the cause of many fights in schools, prison yards, and on the streets. People focus more on the hostile message of the finger-pointing gesture than your verbal statement at that moment.

This is one of the reasons why parents are advised not to use these gestures when communicating with their kids. In addition to that finger-pointing, snapping your fingers in people's faces is regarded as disrespectful and rude.

High-Confidence Hand Display

These hand displays reflect the high degree of assurance and self-confidence an individual is feeling. Here are a few high-confidence hands displays to watch out for in people.

Insecure Hand Displays

Here's a counterpart to the high-confidence hand displays. The low-confidence or insecure hand displays are accurate reflections of the brain's insecurity, discomfort, and self-doubt. So let's examine some hand behaviors that reflect this state.

Frozen Hands

According to research, liars tend to show fewer nonverbal gestures than honest people. When we lie or feel cornered or insecure, we tend to move less or perhaps freeze in order not to draw attention.

It's very easy to detect frozen hands since the person's hand gestures become restrained while telling a lie. So, look out for these restrained hand gestures since they reveal a lot about what's going on in the person's brain.

Hand Wringing

It is usually a sign of stress or low confidence when people interlace their fingers or wring their hands. These are the common responses people use to calm themselves when they feel under stress, threatened, or have low confidence about a situation. The hand-wringing increases in intensity as issues get worse or difficult.

Hand Rubbing

We tend to rub the palms of our hands together when they feel cold; it is a way to warm them up. The lower the temperature, the faster the intensity of the hand rubbing.

This hand gesture is also used by those who are in doubt or under stress. Rubbing the hands together is a way of reassuring or pacifying the brain from doubts and negative emotions that you feel. As the situation escalates, an individual will progress from hand rubbing to interlocking of the fingers.

Emphatic Gestures

How often do we say, "If I were you," and I mean in reality, "If I, I were in one place like yours...?" It's not easy to feel what it's like in someone else's shoes. What do you think of the following rule?

Someone who cannot become aware of their own body language signals will never be able to register the signals of others very accurately. Body language analysis requires not only a "sharp" (read: trained) gaze and a "good" (i.e. trained) ear, but probably a much higher degree of good "sense."

This word describes a good empathy without which any method of self and human knowledge will fail. (You may also know someone who has attended 30 seminars and has read 500 books on the subject and yet does not get beyond a certain limit?) Registering one's own feelings and non-verbal signals means going through two essential processes:

First, one perceives a signal, e.g. For example, one tugs nervously on the lip. Second, you register how you feel right now. This combination helps one later tote others guess what feeling may have triggered a certain signal with them. Of course, this guessing is commonly called 'interpret' because it sounds 'scientific'. However, the fact remains that scientists must also "guess" as long as they work on a theory of knowledge, that is, create. Empathy for others can, therefore, be practiced by registering one's own processes. We can express this again as a rule:

The more empathy a person has with their own emotional world, the more they will be able to develop for others.

And vice versa. This rule also explains why especially sensitive people not only much understanding for others but are also overly sensitive (sometimes mimosa-like) to others. Suggestive Gestures

Suggestive Gestures

Studies show that the way you hold your palms will say a lot about you.

When you have your palms facing upwards, you will show a positive behavior while palms facing downwards will show negative behavior.

Palms facing up tell the person that you are welcoming and honest.

For example, if you are negotiating with a salesperson when buying something and he is putting his palms facing upwards while saying he cannot go any lower than he is honest, and you need to believe him.

If the palms are facing downwards, then he is more emphatic.

It has also been known that those who talk without gesticulating are prone to talking lies than those that talk with a lot of gestures.

If you have watched a politician talk, then you must have realized that they usually use a lot of gestures than many people.

They also like to use open arm gestures to show some honesty.

Pointing is rare in most cases with politicians because they know that it is seen to be rude.

Prompting Gestures

Verbal and nonverbal cues determine how well you can communicate with people. It is about understanding the content and the context at the same time and communicating back in kind. Verbal cues are simple prompts in conversation that ask for your attention or need your response to something. They are very clear.

"Does anyone have the answer?"

This is a direct verbal cue prompting anyone who might have the correct answer to speak up. Everyone understands this. If you don't have the answer, you might probably look around the room to see who has so that you can be attentive and listen to their explanation. Verbal cues are straightforward and explicit. You cannot mistake them.

Direct verbal cues are clear, whether you are asking a question or giving instructions. The message is clear between the decoder and the sender of the message. There is a chronological order in which ideas are conveyed.

The difference with nonverbal cues? These are indirect. They are often implied but not explicit. Indirect verbal cues can be subtle. You have to be very keen to identify them. Given their complicated nature, they are often easy to misunderstand.

Indirect verbal cues are often affected by context. Instead of saying what they want, someone acts it out, hoping you can understand them without them having to say it out loud. Affiliation to different cultural groups, societies, and other interactions often affect the understanding of indirect verbal cues. It might not be easy to read verbal cues, but with some insight, you can hack it. Here are some useful tips:

Recognize Differences. You must first understand that people are different, and for this reason, their communication styles might not be similar to yours. Everyone responds to verbal cues differently. When you respect this, it is easier to create an environment where you can understand one another.

Overcoming Bias. The next thing you have to overcome is your personal bias. Everyone is biased over something in one way or the other. Most of the time, you are biased without even realizing it. This is because of inherent traits, beliefs, and core values that you live by. These affect the way you comprehend things or how you recognize challenges.

Some people who are used to direct verbal cues might find it difficult to interact with people who are used to indirect verbal cues. You might even assume them dishonest because they are not communicating in a manner you are used to. On their part, they might find you unassuming, difficult to deal with, and insensitive. Some might even feel offended, yet you both mean well.

Embrace Diversity. Effective communication is about embracing diversity. People show different emotions in different ways in different parts of the world. This might not be the same as what you are used to, but it is how they do things. It is wise to learn about cultural relations, especially if you might have a very diverse audience.

Practice. You can learn everything you don't know. Learning means setting aside time to practice and get used to people, styles, and so forth. Learning will help you to become flexible and understand the differences between your preferred style of communication and another person's.

Chapter 6 Face

Facial Expressions

Your face is only one small part of your body, but it has a massive impact on what people will be able to pick up from you. While your face might be smaller than something like your stomach or the rest of your body as a whole, it's still an important part that can express a lot of very crucial signals to the person that you're communicating with. People will often look at your face more than anything. They want to look in your eyes, at your mouth and get a better understanding of what you're trying to share. Let's take a look at all the ways that your facial expressions can share greater truth about you in yourself.

Importance of Eyes

We say that the eyes are a window into the soul. That's pretty true; our eyes give a ton of information away about us. Most animals will communicate through eye contact. Our eyes are the one thing that we use to see what's around us and how we pick up on different situations. Let's first discuss what looking up might mean.

How many times have you simply looked up, but somebody else accused you of rolling your eyes? This can be a sign of discomfort. Our eyes will look for the things that are the most interesting around us. If you're having a more challenging conversation and you start to shift your eyes back and forth. When a person looks up, it can often be because they're only looking for more information. They're looking around themselves, trying to either escape the situation by picking up on something to change the subject, or they're searching their brain for more knowledge to include in this interaction.

Looking up can also indicate that we might be trying to recall different types of information. Looking to the left or right could give a signal to the other person that we are lying.

The squinting of the eyes means that we might be trying to focus on something a little more precisely. You'll have to look at the gaze and how long it might be so that people can better understand what the intention of that glare might be. Frequently, we are just like kids are like animals where if we see something shiny or pretty out of the corner of our eyes, we're going to look. It's just a natural human instinct to want to see things that are around us. To use positive eye movements on other people, you can try to notice glances. You might glance at something across the room that you want them to look at as well. Our eyes do a lot of talking to the other person without us even realizing it. If you look at something across the room, then they might be more likely to look at it as well. Alternatively, think about how somebody else might look across the room, and then you also look in that same direction. It's merely a way of our minds thinking that there's something more attractive now than when you got in the room.

Even subtle glances that are less than a second can be an indication that somebody is thinking about something else. For example, if you're having a conversation with somebody and they glance rather quickly right at the front door, then it could be a sign that they're getting bored and that they want to leave. They might look at a clock because they're feeling as though time is passing too slowly. They might glance down with their hands because they're not interested in what you're talking about and are trying to distract themselves.

Pay attention to how people use their eyes, but also consider where they're looking in the context of the location so you can better understand the intention of their eyes.

Micro expressions

Micro expressions are tiny little features within our face that give us a better indication of what somebody else might be thinking or wanting to do. Whether it's a small wrinkle in their forehead or the way that they move their mouth, we can start to pick up on these tiny micro expressions to better understand what somebody is really thinking inside their head.

There are seven different emotions that we can pick up through micro expressions. These include anger, fear, disgust, sadness, content, happiness, and surprise.

These micro expressions will show people in different ways. However, there are specific indications that we can use, which will help us better understand what somebody might be feeling.

Let's first discuss anger. Anger is something that we can pick up on by the way that a person uses their eyebrows and their mouth.

If eyebrows are pointed down and inwards towards the nose, then this is a sign of anger. The lower lid might also become raised up and closing over their eyes, in a way that makes their lives look a little bit more squinted. They'll often keep their lips sucked in and tight around their mouths.

They might have a frown in the way that their cheeks are tense, and their mouths are pointing downwards. Let's move on then to discuss something that we do when something might smell bad, or if we simply don't like the information that somebody is telling us.

We can show disgust in the same kind of way that we do anger in terms of eyebrow usage. Disgust will often leave the person with their mouth hanging open a little bit more. They'll have tense cheeks and a wrinkled nose. Their face is basically recoiling away from the disgusting thing that they're hearing.

Fear is going to have similar eyebrow movements as well. However, they'll be raised extremely high and flat.

If somebody's forehead is wrinkled, and their mouth is slightly open, then this can also tell us that they are feeling fear. Look at the rest of their body to indicate if it's fear, or if it's just surprise. Surprise looks a lot like fear but a little bit more positively. When somebody is surprised, they'll have curved eyebrows versus flat eyebrows as when they're fearful. They'll have their mouth open, but they might have the corners of their mouth turned up a little bit as well.

Even when we receive bad news, we can still sometimes have a smile. The smile might manifest simply because we're trying to work through that emotion in our brain. Sadness is like anger turned downwards. You'll have those arched eyebrows; except they'll be hanging a little bit looser and closer to your eyes.

A more relaxed cheek is seen in sadness, but the corners of their mouth will also be turned down. Content is sort of like complacency. You're satisfied with the moment, but you're not necessarily happy. You feel comfortable, and you're not really angry or anything like that. Content is when we keep our mouths flat. You might have one side or the other raised. Not in a smile just sort of half expression.

This is because we don't have that much emotion at the moment, but we're trying to show the other person what that emotion might be in our face.

The Influence of Smiles

Fake smiling is frequent because it's a way to make the other person know that we're okay with what's going on, but we might not necessarily fully be feeling that emotion.

You can tell somebody is fake smiling by what their eyes look like. Somebody who is fake smiling is not going to have any wrinkles in their eyes, and their eyebrows are going to be completely normal. Somebody who is genuinely smiling will have slightly raised eyebrows and lines in the corners of their eyes.

While their mouth might look the exact same, it's the top of their face that you can use to determine whether somebody's smile is genuine or not.

There are some studies that show that smiling can make you look younger, thinner, and generally like a more exciting person. Those who smile more might actually live longer. We need to conduct more research to really determine if this is the truth or if it's just coincidence. However, some research has helped us realize that people do tend to have longer lifespans based on how much more they might be smiling.

When somebody is smiling, and their mouth is slightly open, then you know that they're thrilled. However, if they're smiling and their mouth is free, and they are genuinely using their eyes, it could be a sign of fear or anxiety. They might be feeling comfortable, but they're using a smile to try to suit the situation. What we have to understand about smiles more than anything else, is that the other person might not be actually that happy but they're at least letting us know that they're feeling generally good. A smile can be a potent tool so you should learn all the ways you can show one. Practice smiling in the mirror to make it look more genuine. Fake smiling isn't always the greatest if you're in a personal relationship. However, a smile can really help in a business and professional setting, it makes everybody feel better, more relaxed, calmer, and more collected (Selig, 2016).

Head Movements

Your head is one of the most critical parts of your body. It has your brain inside of it after all. At the same time, our head can tell us a ton about how we might be feeling. Notice the way that somebody uses their head when they're talking to you.

A head turned downwards can be a way of actually protecting your neck and your chin from getting hurt. It can be a subconscious way of protecting the jugular to make sure that no outside threat could kill you. This is done sometimes when we might be angry, sad, or fearful in general as a way of trying to protect ourselves. Notice the idea that someone is using their eyes when they might be turning their head down as well. If their head is down and they're looking up at you, then they might simply just be tired and want to rest. If their head is down and they're looking from left to right, it can be a sign of fear. If their head is down and they're looking down, it might be a sign that they're sad or depressed.

Notice the way that they turn their heads too. Our leaders can tell us a lot about what is most interesting to us, though we might often turn our entire bodies towards the thing that is causing intrigue.

Somebody who's tilting their head from side to side might also be showing you that they're interested in what you're talking about. They can also be trying to make you feel more comfortable and using it as a way to be a little bit more flirtatious. Nodding or shaking is another powerful way that we use our heads. Those who bow in approval will frequently be in agreement with what you're saying.

Disapproval is going to be from left to right. Even if somebody is actively saying, "Yes," they agree out loud, they might still be nodding their head up and down. It could be a sign of encouragement and that we are still in approval.

But if it's left to right, then it might be a sign of their true feelings that they're trying to hide from you again. Consider cluster movements and notice the head in conjunction with micro expressions. This will give you the most authentic insight into how somebody might be trying to use their body.

Chapter 7 Voice

Tone

The tone, volume, pitch, and emphasis of a person's voice can help you decode the hints that can help you tell what they are feeling. For example, if you notice plenty of inconsistencies in the tone of their voice as they speak, they are probably very angry, hurt, excited, or nervous. Ever notice how your voice shakes when you speak in a rage or are nervous about something? It can also be a sign the person is lying.

Similarly, if a person is speaking louder or softer than their regular volume, something may be amiss. Again, a person's tone is a dead giveaway. Sometimes people say something that sounds like a compliment. However, upon examining their tone closely, you realize the sarcasm and the condescension with which it was uttered.

The tone in which an individual ends their sentence says a lot about what they are trying to convey even with similar verbal clues. For example, if a person completes their sentence on a raised note, they are doubtful of something or are asking a question. Similarly, if they finish the sentence with a flat tone, they are pronouncing a statement or judgment. Watch out for how people end their sentences to get a clue about their inner feelings.

Again, the words people emphasize can help you uncover their true feelings. For example, if a person says, "Have you borrowed the blazer?" while emphasizing 'borrowed,' it indicates their doubt over whether you have borrowed, stolen, or done something else to the blazer. However, if the emphasis is on 'you,' they aren't sure if it is you or someone else who has borrowed the blazer.

I also like to look at pauses between phrases to know about the person's attitude, emotions, and intentions.

For example, if a person pauses after saying something, it could be because what they just said is extremely important to them, or they truly believe in it. Sometimes, a person pauses to seek validation or feedback from others. The speaker wants to gauge your reaction to what they said since it is important for them.

When people are in a more emotionally unstable or negative frame of mind (angry, hurt, or upset), their voice tends to be higher pitched or squeaky. They are most likely losing a grip on their emotions or aren't able to regulate their emotions effectively, notice how, when people are very angry, their voice becomes more screechy and squeakier, as if they are about to cry.

The speed of a speech

A person's emotions clearly impact the speed of their speech. Notice how you start talking much faster than your normal rate of speech, or words per minute, when you are angry or upset. A rapid speech can convey lack of organization, uncertainty, or lack of clarity. The person is not very comfortable with speaking and is just trying to finish throwing his or her words. Again, a slower than usual pace translates into low self-confidence, inability to express emotions, inability to come to terms with one's emotions, lack of emotional reassurance, and other similar feelings.

Chapter 8 Universal Non-verbal Signs

Non-verbal communication will be different for everyone, and it is in different cultures. A person's cultural background will define their non-verbal communication because some types of communication, such as signals and signs, have to be learned.

Because there are various meanings in non-verbal communication, there can be miscommunication could happen when people of different cultures communicate. People might offend another person without actually meaning to because of the cultural differences. Facial expressions are very similar around the world.

There are seven micro-expressions that are universal, and they are content/hate, surprise, anger, fear, disgust, sadness, and happiness. It could also be different to the extent of how people show these feelings because, in certain cultures, people might openly show them where others don't.

You are an American, and you take a trip to Italy. You don't speak Italian. You don't take a translator with you, and you forgot your translation dictionary. You have to rely on non-verbal communication in order to communicate with others.

You found a nice quiet restaurant you want to try so you point at your selection on the menu. You pay your bill and leave. The workers nod at you as you leave being a satisfied customer.

There could be other times when things won't go as well due to non-verbal communication such as people not making eye contact, or they get offended when you do make eye contact.

Nods could also have various meanings, and this causes problems. Some cultures their people might not say "yes," but people from a different culture will interpret as "no."

If you nod in Japan, they will interpret it as you are listening to them.

Here are different non-verbal communications and how they differ in various cultures:

- Physical Space

People in various cultures will have different tolerances for the space between people. People from the Middle East like to be close together when they talk to others. Other people could be afraid to be close to others while talking.

Americans and Europeans don't have as much acceptance about people entering what they consider their physical space. This is even less when talking about Asians. Everyone will have their own personal space that they don't want others to enter. There are many cultures where close contact between strangers is very acceptable.

- Paralanguage

The way we speak constitutes what we talk about. Pitch, rhythm, volume, vocal tones, can speak more than what the words are actually expressing. Asian people can keep themselves from shouting because they have been taught from childhood that this isn't acceptable.

This is what is known as vocal qualifiers. Yelling, whining, and crying are vocal characterizations that can change the message's meaning. In certain cultures, giggling is a very bad gesture. There are several emotions that can be expressed through vocal differences but are all a part of a person's paralanguage.

- Facial Expressions

Our faces can show emotions, attitudes, and feelings. Cultures can determine the degree of these expressions. Americans will show emotions more than people from Asia.

Most facial expressions are the same throughout the world, but certain cultures won't show them in public. These meanings are acknowledged everywhere. Showing too much expression can be taken as being shallow in certain places where others take it as being weak.

- Posture and Body Movement

People can get a message or information from the way your body moves. It can show how a person feels or thinks about you. If they don't face you when you are talking, it might mean that they are shy or nervous. It could also show that they really don't want to be talking with you. Other movements such as sitting far away or near someone could show that they are trying to control the environment. They might be trying to show power or confidence.

A person's posture such as sitting slouched or straight can show their mental condition. Having their hands in their pockets could show disrespect in various cultures. If you are in Turkey or Ghana, don't sit with your legs crossed as this is considered offensive.

- Appearance

This is another good form of non-verbal communication. People have always been judged for their appearance. Differences in clothing and racial differences can tell a lot about anyone.

Making you look good is an important personality trait in many cultures. What is thought to be good appearance will vary from culture to culture. How modest you get measured by your appearance.

- Touch

Touch can be considered rude in many cultures. Most cultures view shaking hands as acceptable. Hugs and kissing, along with other touches, are viewed differently in various cultures. Asians are very conservative with these types of communications.

Patting a person's shoulder or head has various meaning in different cultures, too. Patting a child's head in Asia is very bad because their head is a sacred piece of their body. Middle Eastern countries consider people of opposite genders touching as being very bad character traits.

How and where a person is touched can change the meaning of the touch. You have to be careful if you travel to different places.

- Gestures

You have to be careful with thumbs up because different cultures view it differently. Some could see it as meaning "okay" in some cultures but being vulgar in Latin America. Japan looks at is as money.

Snapping your fingers might be fine in some cultures but taken as offensive and disrespectful in others. In certain Middle Eastern countries, showing your feet is offensive. Pointing your finger is an insult in some cultures. People in Polynesia will stick out their tongue when they greet someone, but in most cultures, this is a sign of mockery.

- Eye Contact

Most Western cultures consider eye contact a good gesture. This shows honesty, confidence, and attentiveness. Cultures like Native American, Hispanic, Middle Eastern and Asian don't make eye contact as a good gesture. It is thought to be offensive and rude.

Unlike Western cultures that think it is respectful, others don't think this way. In Eastern countries, women absolutely can't make eye contact with men because it shows sexual interest or power. Most cultures accept gazes as just showing an expression but staring is thought to be rude in many.

Chapter 9 How to Spot Lie

Fact is that only 54% of the lies can be spotted in an accurate manner. Research has also proved that extroverts tell more lies when compared to the introverts and not less than 82% of the lies usually go without being detected.

However, the good news is that people can also improve their abilities for lie detection, maximizing to close to 90% accuracy. The big question here is how to detect that someone is lying. One of the initial steps in this whole process is getting with how someone typically acts, especially when they are speaking.

Basically, this is the process of coming up with known as a baseline. A baseline is essentially how a person acts when they are under non-threatening and just normal conditions. According to the Science of People website, it is basically how a person appears when they are saying the truth. To make it clearer, it might be a bit difficult to tell when a person is not speaking the fact if you are not sure of how they usually act when saying the truth, which, to a wider extent, makes a lot of sense.

However, the techniques that are used to determine if someone is lying can be very confusing. As a matter of fact, these strategies can even be very conflicting. Due to that, it is important to think twice before making an accusation, ensure that you feel more than once about doing it unless it is important to go ahead and find out what happened.

Here are some of the telltale signs that someone is not telling the truth.

The Behavioral Delay or Pause

It begins when you ask someone a question, and you get no reply initially. The person then begins to respond after some delay. There is one big question that should be asked here; how long should the delay extend before it becomes meaningful before it can be regarded as a deceptive sign? It, however, depends on a few factors. You can try this particular exercise on a friend, and ask a question like this, "What were you doing on a day like this six years ago.

After asking that question, you will notice that the person will take an invariable pause before answering the question. This is because it is not a type of question that naturally evokes a fast and immediate answer. Even as the person takes time to think about the question, he might still not be able to give a meaningful response. The next question to ask would be this," Did you rob a cloth shop on this day six years ago?" if they make a pause before giving you the answer you need, then it would be very important to pick the kind of friends you have wisely.

In most cases, there will be no pause, and the person is likely to respond by just saying no and letting the story die.

This is a simple test that tends to drive home the point that the delays should usually be considered out of the church of God. in the context of whether, it is appropriate for the question at hand.

The Verbal or Non-verbal Disconnect

The human brains have been wired in a manner that causes both the nonverbal and the verbal behaviors to match up in a natural manner. So, each time, there is disconnect it is usually regarded as a very important deceptive indicator. A very common verbal or nonverbal disconnect that you should look out for will occur when someone nods affirmatively while giving a "No" answer. It might also occur when a person moves his head from one end to the other when giving a "Yes" answer.

If you were to carry out that mismatch, as an example, to offer a response to a question, then you will realize that you will have to force yourself through the motion that you have. But despite all that, someone who is deceptive will still do it without even giving it a second thought.

There are a number of caveats that have been connected to this type of indicator. First of all, this type of indicator is not applicable in a short phrase or one-word response. Instead, it is only suitable in a narrative response. For instance, consider that a human head might make a quick nodding motion when a person says "No." That is just a simple emphasis and not a disconnect. Second, it is also very important not to forget that a nodding motion does not necessarily mean "Yes' in certain cultures. In such cultures, a side-to-side head motion also does not imply that the person is saying "No."

Hiding the Eyes or the Mouth

Deceptive people will always hide their eyes or mouth when they are not saying the truth. There is a tendency to desire to cover over a given lie, so if the hand of a person moves in front of their mouth while they are making a response to a given question, which becomes significant.

In a similar instance, hiding the eyes can be an inclination to shield a person from the outlast of those they could be lying to. If an individual shield or covers their eyes when they are responding to a question, what they could also be showing, on the level of subconscious, is that they can't bear to see the reaction to the lie they are saying. In most cases, this kind of eye shielding could be done using the hand, or the person could as well decide to close the eyes. Blinking is not in the picture here, but when a person closes their eyes while making a response to a question that doesn't need reflection to answer, which can be considered as a way of hiding the eyes, hence becoming a possible deceptive indicator.

Swallowing or Throat Clearing

If a person loudly swallows saliva or clears the throat before answering a given question, then there is a problem somewhere. However, if any of these actions are performed after they have answered the question, then there is nothing to worry about. But when it happens before answering a question, then there are some things that should be analyzed.

The person could be doing the nonverbal equivalent of the following verbal statements," I swear to God..." This is one of the ways of dressing the lie in the best attires before presenting it. Looking at it from the physiological point of view, the question might have created a type of anxiety spike, which can as well as cause dryness and discomfort in the throat and mouth.

The Hand-to-Face Actions

The other way of determining if someone is saying a lie is to check what they do with their faces or in the head region each time they are asked a question. Usually, this would take the form of licking or biting the lips or even pulling the ears or lips together. The main reason behind this reflects one of the simple science questions that are usually discussed in high school. When you have someone a question, and you notice that it creates a kind of spike in anxiety, what you should remember is that the right response will be damaging. In return, that will activate the autonomic nervous system to get to business and try to dissipate the anxiety, which might appear to drain a lot of blood from the surface of the extremities, ears, and the face. The effects of this could be a sensation of itchiness or cold. Without the person even realizing it, his hands will be drawn to the mentioned areas, and there could be rubbing or wringing of the hands. And just like that, you might have spotted a deceptive indicator.

The Nose Touch

Women usually carry out this special gesture with smaller strokes compared to those of men, as a way of avoiding smudging of their make-ups. One of the most important things to recall is that this kind of action should be read in context and clusters, as the person could have any hay of cold or fever.

According to a group of scientists at the Smell & Taste Treatment and Research Foundation that is based in Chicago, when someone lies, chemicals that are called catecholamine are released and make the tissue that is inside the nose to swell. The scientists applied a special imaging camera that reveals the blood flow in the body and show that deliberate lying can also lead to an increase in the blood pressure. This technology proves that the human nose tends to expand with blood when someone lies, and that is what is referred to as the Pinocchio Effect.

Maximized blood pressure will also inflate the nose and make the nervous nose tingle, leading to a kind of brisk rubbing with the hand to suppress the itching effect.

The swelling cannot be seen with the naked eyes, but it is usually what causes the nose touch gesture. The same phenomenon will also take place when a person is angry, anxious, and upset. American psychiatrist Charles Wolf and neurologist Alan Hirsch carried out a detailed analysis of the testimony of Bill Clinton to the Grand Jury on the affair he had with Monica Lewinsky. They realized that each time he was being honest, he rarely touched his nose. However, when he lied, he offered he appeared to be wearing a frown before he gave the answer and touched his nose once each 4 minutes for a mega total of 26 nose touches. The scientists also said the former US president didn't touch his nose at all when he offered the answers to the questions in a truthful manner.

A deliberate scratching or rubbing action, as opposed to a nose that could just be itching lightly, usually satisfies the itch of someone's nose. Usually, an itch is a repetitive and isolated signal and is out of context or incongruent with the general conversation of the person.

Eye Rub

When a child does not want to see something, the only thing they will do is to cover their eyes. They usually do this with both of their hands. On the other hand, when an adult does not want to see something distasteful to them, they are likely to rub their eyes. The eye is one of the attempts by the brain to block out a doubt, deceit, or any distasteful thing that it sees. It is also done to avoid looking at the face of the person who the lie is being said to. Usually, men would firmly rub their eyes, and they may look away if the myth is a real whopper.

Women are not so likely to use the eye rub gesture. Instead, they will use gentle and small touching emotions just beneath the eyes since they either want to avoid interfering with the makeups they are wearing, or they have been redesigned as girls to stay away from making several gestures. At times, they might also want to avoid the listener's gaze by trying to look away.

One of the commonly used phrases out there is lying through the teeth. It is used to refer to a cluster of gestures portraying fake smile and clenched teeth, accompanied by the famous eye rub.

Chapter 10 Spotting Romantic Interest

Spotting romantic interest is one of the most popular topics of all time. Consistently, both men and women are interested in learning more about how they can determine if a person is genuinely attracted to them.

This topic is part science and part art. There is plenty of scientific evidence that backs up the reasoning behind attraction while there is an instinctive component, which cannot be adequately measured or quantified through scientific methods. What this implies is that if you are looking to gauge someone's level of attraction, then you need to have both a scientific approach and reliance on gut feelings.

To start things off, it should be noted that attraction works differently in men than it does in women. While the underlying biochemistry is essentially the same, the physical manifestations are different. In addition, cultural norms may govern romantic interactions to a varying degree.

In that regard, it is worth mentioning that while many of the non-verbal clues are the same, women tend to be a lot more subtle than men are. In contrast, most men tend to be very open about their feelings toward the object of their attraction. While this shouldn't be taken as a blanket statement, it is a general rule of thumb. After all, there are plenty of shy men out there who have trouble making their interest known while there are plenty of women who are quite overt about their feelings for the object of their interest.

One other note with regard to attraction is that romantic interactions are generally perceived to be between men and women.

That being said, I intend to have this discussion cover the entire spectrum of male and female interaction within a romantic context. That way, the information presented herein will provide you with the insights you need in order to improve your ability to pick up on the non-verbal clues indicating potential romantic interest and attraction.

Now, the first to keep in mind is that attraction is somewhat hard to define. The reason for this is that men and women seek different things in a potential mate. We are operating under the assumption that there is genuine attraction among those involved and not some hidden agenda spurring interest.

In that regard, the attraction is based on the qualities of an individual that meet or exceed the needs of the other. Hence, women tend to focus on different qualities in their potential romantic partner, whereas men tend to focus on a different set of qualities.

For instance, women tend to seek security and stability in a romantic partner. This is due to an instinctive need for survival and preservation of the species. In order to fully comprehend this, we would need to go all the way back to the day of primitive humans in which there was no guarantee that offspring would make it past their first year of life. As such, women, designated as a caregiver from the start, needed to secure the means and resources needed to ensure the survival of their offspring. On the other hand, the males were in charge of playing the role of provider.

In the early days of humankind, males were mainly hunter-gatherers. This means that they needed to go into the fray to find food. Whether food came from hunting or foraging, males were expected to provide the sustenance needed to ensure the survival of their offspring.

In contrast, males needed to find healthy females who had the physical qualities that would ensure their fertility and ability to bear children. I know that this sounds very primitive, but it is important to underscore this point as humans we are hardwired under this context. Consequently, thousands of years of evolution and biology are just now being challenged by the new social paradigm in which we find ourselves.

Over the last two hundred years or so, the dating paradigm has shifted dramatically.

Traditionally, most marriages were arranged. As such, it was not so much about love and romance, but about the position and financial stability. This paradigm lasted for a few centuries. Since the outset of the Industrial Revolution, the attitudes of society changed in such a way that men and women were free to choose who they wanted to marry. This opened the door for a number of circumstances.

So, men went from courting women to dating them. This meant that men needed to ensure that a woman would be willing to reciprocate his intentions and feelings. In contrast, women played a more passive role, and they were conditioned to wait for men to make the first move. However, they could drop subtle hints regarding their interest. That way, the man would be certain that he had a chance with a given woman.

In modern times, we are faced with a very liberal dating scene. While some countries have far more cultural and religious restrictions, most countries are fairly open about the manner in which they can pursue the object of their desire.

Consequently, it is imperative that both men and women gain deeper insight as to how attraction is expressed by either gender.

So, let us start off with men.

Men are a lot easier to read, as they tend to be far more overt about their interest in someone. They will generally seek the object of their interest and engage them in some manner. Typically, men will try to engage the other party by displays of strength, wealth, or status. These are signs that they are providers or protectors. In short, men try to position themselves as the best possible mate their object of interest can find.

Some general guidelines include direct eye contact, tilting their body toward the person they are attracted to and seeking constant physical contact. The latter generally tends to make most women uncomfortable, as unsolicited physical contact can get rather awkward quickly.

Other not so subtle hints that men drop are following the object of their affection around, placing their hands, or arms, as a sign of possession and frequent fidgeting.

In fact, fidgeting is a dead giveaway as it is a sign that a man is nervous in the presence of whom they are attracted to.

In addition, some men might go silent (remember the freeze response?) and even fail to react in the presence of the object of the attraction. This reaction is partially due to the freeze response but it also due to the fact that some men freeze up when they don't know what to do or how to react.

This is why you see most dating advice that is oriented to men focus on what to do and what to say in various situations. What this does is that it eliminates a man's reliance on his wits by providing him with a set of tools. These tools are certainly useful though they may not be universally applicable.

One common method used by men is to approach and pull back. This method consists in approaching someone they are attracted to and then pulling away. Then, they will engage and withdraw until they are able to make progress, say, go on a first date. The logic beneath this approach is that men tend to come on very strong when they are attracted to someone. As such, this approach allows them to find a balance between displaying their intentions and giving the object of their attraction some space.

As you can see, men are far more open about their attraction toward someone based on the permissiveness that society has afforded men throughout history. However, women have been traditionally tagged with a more submissive role. Therefore, women are not always able to express their intentions overtly in the same way that men do.

Some not so subtle signs of attraction in women are eye contact, hair pulling, and trailing off in conversation.

When a woman is attracted to a person, she will seek eye contact. This eye contact tends to be rather brief as women are not interested in winning a staring contest. They just want to signal to the object of their interest that they are willing to be engaged.

Another telltale sign of attraction in a woman is related to her hair. If you see a woman playing or pulling on her hair when speaking to someone they like, you can be pretty sure that she is indicating a willingness to be engaged.

Also, women who are interested in a person will allow for closer physical contact. Any a time a woman keeps people at arms' length, it is a clear indication that they have no interest in them. By the same token, any time a woman avoids eye contact and tilts their body away from the person they is interacting with, it is safe to assume they are not interested in being engaged.

Women are generally focused on faces. What this means is that when a woman is attracted to someone, they will not only focus on their eyes but also their mouth. They generally tend to watch the other party's lips when they speak. This is an instinctive reaction based on their desire to find a strong and healthy mate. Consequently, healthy-looking eyes, teeth, lips, and skin are clear indicators that a person is in good physical condition.

Women also drop many hints with their arms and hands. A woman who is uninterested will almost always cross her arms and/or legs at some point. If you find that a woman is sitting in the manner on a date, then the other party has a tough time ahead for them.

Conversely, if a woman is actually interested in the other person, she will sit, or stand, in a very "open" position, that is, hands at her sides (or folded on a table) and legs uncrossed. Also, leaning forward while listening to the interlocutor is a good indication that they are interested in what the other person has to say. If they make direct eye contact on various occasions, then the combination of clues is virtually a declaration of intent.

Some women refrain from eye contact when they are genuinely attracted to someone. They may cross gazes but quickly look away or perhaps look down. In some cultures, this is the norm, as it is a sign of submission. Western cultures don't normally have such customs though women may still prefer to avoid eye contact in order to prevent themselves from being too obvious.

Finally, a woman's voice says a lot about the way she feels. Women tend to speak with a higher pitch when they are in the presence of someone they are attracted to. Also, they may raise the tone of their voice in order to be "noticed" by the person they are attracted to. In one on one interaction, don't be surprised if you see a woman speaking somewhat faster. However, if she begins to slow down, then that might very well be a signal that she has lost interest.

On the whole, men and women will exhibit very similar signs of attraction such as open lips, rounded eyes, eyebrows higher than usual and the classic pupil dilation (this is actually very hard to spot). However, hands, arms and body positioning are far more indicative of attraction than other signs commonly mentioned.

In addition, facial gestures such as smiling are good indicators though not foolproof. After all, you might be talking with someone who is upbeat and positive. However, that does not mean that they are attracted to you.

Chapter 11 Tips

Tips on How to Improve your Non-verbal Communication

Solid communication abilities can help you in both your own and expert life. While verbal and composed communication abilities are significant, investigate has shown that nonverbal practices make up an enormous level of our everyday relational communication.

How might you improve your nonverbal communication abilities? The accompanying tips can assist you with figuring out how to read the nonverbal signals of others and upgrade your own capacity to impart viably.

Focus on Nonverbal Signals

Individuals can convey data from numerous points of view, so focus on things like eye contact, gestures, posture, body developments, and manner of speaking. These signals can pass on significant data that isn't articulated.

By giving nearer consideration to others' implicit practices, you will improve your own capacity to convey nonverbally.

Search for Incongruent Behaviors

Research has indicated that when words neglect to coordinate with nonverbal signals, individuals will, in general, disregard what has been said and center rather around implicit expressions of states of mind, considerations, and feelings. So when somebody says a certain something, however, their body language appears to recommend something different, it tends to be valuable to give additional consideration to those unpretentious nonverbal signals.

Use Good Eye Contact

Great eye contact is another fundamental nonverbal communication ability. When people neglect to look at others without flinching, it can appear as though they are dodging or attempting to conceal something. Then again, an excessive amount of eye contact can appear to be fierce or threatening.

While eye contact is a significant piece of communication, recall that great eye contact doesn't always mean gazing steadily at someone. How you tell what amount of eye contact is right?

Some communication specialists suggest interims of eye contact enduring four to five seconds. Powerful eye contact should feel normal and agreeable for both you and the individual you are talking with.

Pose Inquiries About Nonverbal Signals

Occasionally, just posing such inquiries can loan a lot of clearness to a circumstance. For instance, an individual may be radiating sure nonverbal signals since he has something different on his mind. By inquisitive further into his message and plan, you may show signs of improvement thought of what he is truly attempting to state.

Use Signals to Make Communication More Meaningful

Recollect that verbal and nonverbal communication cooperate to pass on a message. You can improve your expressed communication by utilizing body language that strengthens and bolsters what you are stating. This can be particularly valuable when making introductions or when addressing an enormous gathering of individuals.

For instance, if you will probably seem sure and arranged during an introduction, you will need to concentrate on imparting nonverbal signs that guarantee that others consider you to be confident and competent. Standing solidly in one spot, shoulder back, and your weight-adjusted on the two feet is an extraordinary method to pause dramatically.

Take a gander at Signals as a Whole

Another significant piece of good nonverbal communication abilities includes having the option to adopt an increasingly all-encompassing strategy to what an individual is conveying. A solitary motion can mean any number of things, or possibly nothing by any means.

The way to precisely reading nonverbal conduct is to search for gatherings of signals that fortify a typical point. In the event that you place an excessive amount of accentuation on only one signal out of many, you may arrive at an off base decision about what an individual is attempting to state.

Think about the Context

At the point when you are speaking with others, generally consider the circumstance and the setting wherein the communication happens. A few circumstances require increasingly formal practices that may be deciphered contrastingly in some other setting.

Be Aware That Signals Can be Misread

As per somewhere in the range of, a confident handshake shows a solid character while a feeble handshake is taken as an absence of backbone. This model outlines a significant point about the plausibility of misreading nonverbal signals. A limp handshake may really show something different completely, for example, joint inflammation.

Continuously make sure to search for gatherings of conduct. An individual's general disposition is unmistakably more telling than a solitary signal saw in disengagement.

Practice, Practice, Practice

A few people simply appear to have a talent for utilizing nonverbal communication successfully and accurately deciphering signals from others. These individuals are regularly depicted as having the option to "read individuals."

As a general rule, you can fabricate this aptitude by giving careful consideration to nonverbal conduct and rehearsing various sorts of nonverbal communication with others. By seeing nonverbal conduct and rehearsing your own aptitudes, you can significantly improve your communication capacities.

Nonverbal communication abilities are fundamental and can make it simpler to pass on your point and to read what others are attempting to let you know. A few people appear to stop by these aptitudes normally, yet anybody can improve their nonverbal abilities with training.

Tips on How to protect yourself from Deception

It is relieving to know that there are defense mechanisms against deception and a person faced with a deceptive situation can always stand against and defend him/herself from it.

According to researchers, pride was one of the major factors that allow people to fall into deception. When a person feels he or she is too good and perfect, or feels he/she can be very careful, then it leaves room for the con agent to take advantage.

Enlightened skepticism is a technique used to defend yourself against deception, there is a saying: "truth fears no questions." This approach protects you from harmful forms of deception, as it is a way to assess the truth through a fact-finding and questioning method. When you do these things, you tend to gain from this effort in at least three ways, which are:

- You tend to hone your critical thinking skills.

- You learn to choose who to trust and to what extent to trust them.

- You get to find out who is after personal advantage at your expense.

In order to risk falling into someone's deceptive trap, researchers have come up with some enlightened skepticism questions that can help you to defend yourself against deception. Some of the questions to ask include:

1. What are the things I know about the person's truthfulness?

2. Is the person's statement consistent with the truth or reality?

3. Is there a way to verify or check the authenticity of the statement?

4. What do I stand to gain if I accept and act on the statement?

5. And if I don't gain, what would I lose if I accept and act on the statement?

6.   What is the gain of the speaker if I buy into the statement?

7.   Is there any part of the statement exaggerated or downplayed by the speaker?

8.   Does the idea seem or sound too good to be true?

9.   Would I advise my close relation to accept the statement without an iota of doubt?

10.   What doesn't feel right?

These 10 questions make you more objective and allow you to think critically when receiving information. When you ask and answer these questions there is a lesser chance that you will be fooled since you will come across as sincere and sharp and this will ward off deceivers as they will move on in search of easier targets.

Just like simulations occur in deception, there is also simulation in defending or warding off the deception. These deception detection skills come with some fun simulations, some of which includes:

Talk shows on TV:

Listening to people argue about different topics. Pick out the truth, the exaggerations and half-truths told by a speaker in the process of making his/her point. Also, look out for outright lies, emotional reasoning, fallacies and all other deceptive behavior. Being able to identify these things allow you to get better at detecting deception.

Commercials: These also gives you opportunities to work more on your critical thinking skills. In advertisements there are a lot of mistakes in reasoning, arguments based on things without facts, a lot of lies and deception. Being able to detect this will improve your ability to detect a deceptive person from a distance.

If you can find the flaws in simulated information, hold on with judgment until you have enough information to render a reasonable accusation. It is only at this point that you can say that you have truly mastered the act of deceptive defense.

But again, a person who is good at defending him or herself from deception is only as good as the agent of deception he/she is faced with. Some people tend to be more skilled at lying and constant interaction and simulation are the only way to improve on one's deception detection.

Chapter 12 Deception

The method of mind control will have some parallels with manipulation in that manipulators will use a lot of deception to achieve their ultimate goal..

Deception is an act used by the agent to spread ideas in the object regarding facts that are falsehoods or that are just partial truths, along with subterfuge, mystification, hoax, provocation, and beguilement. Deception may include many different things like concealment, disguise, distraction, hand sleight, manipulation, and concealment. The agent will be able to control the subject's mind because the subject will trust them. The subject may believe what the agent says and may even base future plans and shape their life on the things the agent told them. Deception also happens in terms of relationships.

Types of Deception

Deception is a form of communication that relies on omissions and lies to persuade the subject to best fit the object of the environment. As contact is involved, several different types of deception may also occur. There are five different types of deception found, according to the Interpersonal Deception Theory. In the other forms of mind control, some of these have been seen, suggesting that there may be some overlap. The five main forms of deception are:

Lies: This is when the agent compiles data and provides information that is totally different from what the truth is. They can present that information as fact to the subject and the subject will see it as the truth. This can be risky, as the subject does not know that they are being fed false information; if the subject knew that the information is inaccurate, they would certainly not speak to the agent and there would be no deceit.

Equivocations: This is when the agent makes statements that are inconsistent, vague and indirect. This is intended to get the subject confused and not to understand what is happening. If the subject returns later and tries to blame them for the false information, it can also allow the agent to save face.

Concealments: This is one of the most commonly used forms of deception. Concealments are when the agent intentionally omits data relevant or important to the context and participates in any actions that would hide information relevant to the subject for that particular context. The agent is not likely to have lied explicitly to the subject, but they are going to make sure that the important information required never makes it to the subject.

Exaggeration: This is when the agent overestimates a fact or subtly twists the facts to turn the story the way they want. While the agent may not be lying explicitly to the subject, they are going to make the situation look like a bigger deal than it really is or they are going to change the reality a little so that the subject does what they want.

Understatements: An underestimate is the exact opposite of the method of exaggeration because the agent would downplay or diminish aspects of the reality. They are going to tell the subject that an event is not that big deal when it could actually be the thing that determines whether the subject gets to graduate or gets that big promotion.

These are just a few of the possible types of deception.

Motives for Deception

Researchers have shown that there are three main motives that are present in deceptions found in close relationships. These would include partner-focused motives, self-focused motives, and relationship focused motives.

Deception techniques

Camouflage

This is when the agent acts in a certain way to hide the truth so that the subject does not know that the information is missing. Often when the agent uses half-truths as they say information, it strategy will be used.

Disguise

The agent works to create the illusion of being something or someone else when this occurs. It is when the agent hides everything about themselves from the topic including their real name, what they are doing for a career, whom they have been with, and what they are up to when they go out. This goes beyond simply changing the outfit that someone wears in a play or film; when disguise is used in the process of deception, the agent attempts to change their entire persona to confuse and mislead the subject.

Simulation

It consists in displaying fake subject data. In simulation, there are three methods that can be used like deception, manufacturing, or mimicry. The agent may unintentionally represent something identical to itself in mimicry, and copying another template. They may have an idea similar to someone else's and they will assume it is all theirs instead of giving credit. By auditory, visual and other means, it type of simulation can often occur.

Fabrication is another method that can be used by the agent when using deception. What this means is that the agent is going to take something that is actually found and change it to be different. They can tell a story that has not happened or added to embellishments that make it sound better or worse than it was. While the core of the story may be true, yes, they got a bad grade on a test; some extra things are going to be put in as the teacher purposefully gave them a bad grade. The truth is that the agent has not been training, and that is why they first got the bad score.

Finally, in deception, distraction is another type of simulation. This is when the agent tries to get the target to focus their attention on something other than the facts; typically by baiting or providing something more enticing than the hidden truth.

Did I see ways in which I can improve in order to master or break free from one or more, if possible all 5 forms of dark psychology?

Have I outlined the necessary line of action to take?

Do I possess the discipline to stick to the line of action I have outlined?

If I should experience some shortcomings in following my outlined goals, how can I quickly get back on track?

Chapter 13 Body Language of Attraction

You may be insanely attracted to a person but may not have the courage to ask them out owing to the prospect of facing humiliation and rejection. Imagine how easier things would be if you knew if they are as much into you as you are into them. Think of a situation where you've been set up on a blind date by enthusiastic friends, or you find a date online, and really want to know if they are attracted to you. You may go out on a first date and come back not knowing whether the person really liked you or not!

Wouldn't it be nice if there could be a telepathic way to gauge if a person feels truly attracted to you? How can you figure out if a person is genuinely attracted to you or is being plain nice to you because they don't want to hurt you (yes, we've all been guilty of this.)

Can verbal and non-verbal clues help you establish a potential lover's true feelings, emotions, thoughts, and intentions? Can body language be used for unlocking a person's subconscious mind to tune in to their innermost feelings and thoughts about you? Use these secret attraction clues (that I rarely share with anyone) to help you gain and increase social proof and experience more gratifying and fulfilling relationships.

The Attraction Signals

When an individual is attracted to you, they will transmit plenty of feel-good or positive non-verbal clues for you to tune in to at a subconscious level.

To begin with, when a person is deeply attracted to you, their bodies will almost always face you.

Everything from their face, the chest to shoulders and feet will most likely be pointed in your direction. The person will lean closer while speaking or interacting with you in a bid to get closer on a subconscious and emotional level. When they stand at a distance of under four feet away from you, they are keen on entering or personal space or inner circle of friends. They are trying to physically enter your inner zone or personal space to make a place for themselves in it.

If you want to know if a person is keenly into you or interested in you, don't give in to their interest straight away. Rather than facing them, maintain a shoulder to shoulder position. If the person is truly interested in you, he or she will make an effort to win your attraction. Let them know that they have to win your attraction for you to stand facing them or mirror their attraction signals.

Leaning in the direction of a person is almost always a sign of attraction. We subconsciously lean towards people we are attracted to. When a person leans towards you in a group, it is clear that they are interested in you (or what you are speaking). Of course, sometimes a person may be simply keen on listening to what you are saying, in which case, you will have to look at other clues. However, leaning towards a person within a group setting is a subconscious indication that they are drawn towards you.

Another sign of attraction includes seizing a person from up to down, and then down to up. This is a primitive way, yet still practiced, for checking out the sexual potential of a prospective mate.

Together with other clues, uncrossed arms and legs can be a sign of attraction. Similarly, a broad smile, dilated pupils, and open palms can also reveal attraction. Head tilting is another sign of interest and engagement. It signals a person's desire to communicate to you that they are always around for you. Looking at a person in the eye for long while speaking can also be a huge sign of attraction. If you are attracted to a person or want to win their affection, avoid looking over their heads or even all over the place. It reveals a lack of interest and sensitivity, which will not give them the right signal.

Touch

Touch is a clue that an individual is completely comfortable in your presence. They may also be keen or getting to know more about you. They may get flirtatious or hit on you by playfully touching you. Some of the most common initial attractions signals are placing their hand over your hand, brushing their shoulder or leg against your shoulder or leg while talking to you and pretending to touch you accidentally.

If you are confused about how to read a person's touches, observe how they touch another person versus how they touch you. If they are generally touchy-feely with everyone around, it is their baseline personality.

However, if they make special exceptions in the manner in which they touch you, it is more often than not, a sign of attraction. If the individual touches more than normal or in a different way, he or she may be attracted to you.

If you are attracted to a person, use body language to your advantage by conveying your feelings through non-verbal signals. Don't distance yourself from the person even if you don't want to send out very obvious signs of attraction.

On a subconscious level, they may not realize they are attracted to you. Similarly, don't go all out and make the person step back in discomfort. Maintain a balance. Start with a light or playful tap on the shoulder or elbows. It is harmless yet reveals that a person likes you. Then gradually, move to touch their arm, wrist or back while talking. Make the touch more gradual and subtle so they don't wince or retreat with discomfort.

Mirroring

Mirroring happens at a deeply subconscious level and is one of the most reliable signals of a person's attraction. Watch out for people mirroring your actions.

There is either a deep-seated need to be accepted or they are truly attracted to you. Sometimes after you've just met or been introduced to a person at a party, you'll notice that he or she starts mirroring everything from your words to your nods to your hand gestures to expressions.

People who don't know much about reading or analyzing people will often miss these clues.

However, on a subconscious level, this is a sign that the person is seeking your acceptance or approval. When you are leaning against the bar, you'll notice a person come up to you and lean in the same position as you before striking up a conversation. They are doing nothing but attempting to mirror your actions in a bid to make you feel that they are one among your kind. People will hold their glass exactly in the manner in which you are holding yours or they may take a sip on their drink right after you do to show you that they are like you. The feeling of affiliating with people on a psychological level drives people to mirror their actions.

Chapter 14 Mirroring

Have you ever sat in a restaurant and people watched? It can be quite amusing to sit back and watch all of the people out and about around you, attempting to identify how their relationships must be going by body language alone. Yes, it is quite possible to understand at the briefest glance at another how they get along. You can absolutely tell how much or how little people get along simply by watching them together and seeing how they naturally orient their bodies around each other. This simple skill is referred to as mirroring, and it is absolutely crucial if you want to be successful at influencing or persuading others. When you understand mirroring, you essentially have a built-in system in which you can judge just how well people are likely to be willing to listen to you. You can tell if you are successful in developing rapport, and if you have not, you will be able to push the act of earning rapport along a little quicker. You can utilize mirroring in a wide range of ways that can absolutely be beneficial to you, and you can utilize it in ways that can be useful to others as well.

What is Mirroring?

First things first, you must learn what mirroring is. At the simplest, it is the human tendency to mirror what is happening around them when they feel a relationship to whatever it is that is around them. For example, if you look at an old married couple, they are likely to constantly be mirroring each other's behaviors. It is essentially the ultimate culmination of empathy—the individuals are so bonded, so aware of each other and their behaviors, that they unconsciously mimic any behaviors that their partner does first. The two married people at the diner may both sip at their coffees at the same time as each other, or if one drinks, the other will follow shortly after. If one shifts in his seat, she will do so as well, always leaning to mirror the position her husband is in. If she brushes off something on her shoulder, he will unconsciously touch his shoulder as well. This act is known as mirroring, and it occurs in a wide range of circumstances.

You do not necessarily have to be a married couple that has been together for decades for mirroring to be relevant, either—you can see it everywhere. The person interviewing you for a job may begin to mirror you when the interview is going well, or the person who thinks that you are attractive may mimic some of your behaviors as well. You can see these behaviors mimicked started quite early on in terms of how long people have been interacting as well—sometimes people will even hit it off right off the bat and begin mirroring each other, emphasizing the fact that they seemed to have clicked.

Mirroring is essentially the ultimate form of flattery—it involves literally copying the other person because you like or love them so much. Children mirror their parents when learning how to behave in the world. Good friends often mirror each other. Salespeople wanting to win rapport, mirror people. No matter what the relationship is, if it is a positive one, there are likely mirroring behaviors, whether unconscious or not.

Uses of Mirroring

You may be wondering why something as simple as mimicry can actually be important to others, but it is actually one of the most fundamental parts of influence, persuasion, and manipulation. When you mirror someone, you can develop rapport. Rapport is essentially the measurement of your relationship with someone—if you have a good rapport with someone, you have developed some level of trust with them. The other person is likely to believe what you are saying if you develop rapport. However, if you have not yet developed rapport yet and you need the other person to listen to you, you can oftentimes artificially create that rapport through one simple task—mirroring. If you mirror the other person, you can essentially convince him to develop a rapport with you, whether it was something he wanted to develop on his own or whether you forced the point.

By constantly mirroring the other person, you essentially send the signs to their brain that they need to like this person because this person is just like them. Remember the three key factors for likability? The first one was able to relate or identify with the other person. In this case, you are presenting yourself as easy to relate to simply because you want the other person to like you. With liking you comes rapport. With rapport comes trust, which you can use to convince the other person to buy cars or do certain things that will benefit you. Building rapport even builds up the ability to be able to manipulate the other person—you need to be trustworthy for the other person to let you close enough to manipulate in the first place.

How to Mirror

Luckily for you, mirroring is quite easy to learn how to do. While it may seem awkward and unnatural at first, the more you practice it, the more natural it will become to you, and the more effective you can get at it. Remember, if you want to mirror someone, you will need to toe the line between too much and not enough. If you are too overt, the other person will catch on and will likely be more put off than convinced to like you. Take a look at these four steps so you can learn to mirror for yourself.

Build up a Connection

The first step when you are attempting to mirror someone is to start by building a connection somehow. If you do not feel the connection with the other person, they are not likely to be feeling a connection either. Keeping that in mind, you should begin to foster some sort of connection and rapport. This can be done with four simple steps on its own.

Fronting: This is the act of facing the other person entirely. You start with your body oriented toward them, directly facing the other person to give them your complete attention.

Eye contact: This is the tricky part—when you are making eye contact, you need to make sure that you get the right amount.

The triple nod: This does two things—it encourages the other person to keep speaking because the other person feels valued and listened to, and it makes the other person feel like you agree with them. It develops what is known as a yes set. The more you say yes, the more likely you are to develop a connection with the other person.

Fake it till you make it: At this point, you have spent a lot of time setting up the connection, and it is time for the moment of truth. You should imagine that the person is the most interesting in the world at that particular moment. You want to really believe that they are interesting to you. Then stop pretending—you should feel that they are actually interesting to you at this point. This is the birth of the connection you had been trying to establish.

Pace and Volume

Now, before you start mimicking their body language, start by paying attention to the other person's vocal cues. You want to make sure you are speaking at the same speed as the other person. If they are a quick speaker, you should also speak quickly, and if they are a slower speaker, you should slow your own speaking pace down to match. From there, make sure you are also mimicking the volume. If they are louder, you should raise your own voice. If they are keeping their voice down, you should follow suit. These vocal cues are far easier to mimic undetected than the rest of the physical cues.

The Punctuator

Everyone has a punctuator they use for emphasis. It could be something like a hand gesture that is used every time they want to emphasize something, or it could be the way they raise their brows as they say the word they want to stress. No matter what the punctuator is, you should identify what it is and seek to mimic it at the moment. Now, oftentimes, this cue is entirely unconscious on the other person's part, and as you begin to mimic it, the other person is likely to believe that you are on the same wavelength. This should really do it for you without making what you are doing obviously.

The Moment of Truth

Now, you are ready to test whether you have successfully built up the rapport you need. When you want to know if the other person has officially been connected to you, you should make some small action that is unrelated to what you are doing at that particular moment and see if the other person does it back. For example, if you are having a conversation about computers, you may reach up and rub your forehead for a split second. Watch and see if the other person also rubs at their forehead right after you. If they do, they have connected to you, and you can begin to move forward with your persuasive techniques.

Chapter 15 Body Language Applications

Body language and self-esteem go hand in hand. This allows for a wonderful mechanism to observe and monitor how people behave and feel. Awareness of our body language is essential for becoming effective and persuasive communicators. Hence, there are several applications for using, reading, and changing body language.

Therapeutic Applications

Body language plays a major role in counseling, NLP, and hypnotherapy. For psychologists, body language not only allows them a way to read their clients' emotional state, but also gives them a way to build rapport. Observing the client's body language can help the psychologist to read how the client responds to a certain discussion or line of questioning.

Body language speaks when we can't. Health care professionals have known this for some time. A great many studies have been conducted in it, and psychology academic studies for professionals including modalities on body language.

Common issues which can be examined and treated through the use of body language include:

Bi polarity

Individuals with this condition suffer a chemical imbalance that leads to severe depression and the inability to make decisions. They often have a low self-esteem that accompanies this disorder, and it is incredibly difficult to understand effectively or treat correctly. Using body language, the person with bipolarity can be taught to manage their daily situations, and considering the link between body language and emotion, they can also enjoy relief by being trained to use positive body language. This is a way for them to use their own body language to persuade their emotions to stabilize and improve. For their families, body language reading is also an effective way to monitor their loved one's state and intervene before incidents happen. Depression can often go unnoticed and people will rarely speak out about it. They are not likely to say: "I'm feeling depressed."

Low self-esteem

Many of us have suffered the devastating effects of low self-esteem in one way or another. The first victim is our ability to progress in life. A positive belief in yourself is needed if you are to convince the rest of the world to believe in you. People can be trained in positive body language such as the open position, making eye contact, lifting the head. It's a case of faking it until you feel it. With enough repetitive use of persuasive body language, you can even convince yourself that you are stronger than you believe.

Trauma

Survivors of trauma suffer from a loss of power, feelings of inadequacy, and loss of confidence. They also have the burden of guilt where they hold themselves responsible for what happened to them. Whether the trauma is due to a violent act such as an assault or rape, a natural disaster or loss in their family, the emotional state of these individuals is reflected in their body language or the change thereof. Where body language may have been positive and inviting before the incident, the person may now display negative body language, such as crossed arms, slumping, excessive facial touching, and nervous ticks such as repetitive movement. With effective counseling, their progress to recovery can be tracked through counseling and monitoring their body language.

Abuse

Abuse can be physical, emotional, and sexual in nature, but whichever of these it is, there is bound to be an overwhelming sense of a loss of power. The victim may need to be convinced that they can regain their power and that it is okay to trust people. Body language is extremely efficient in this regard. Helping these survivors of abuse establish strong body language will increase their sense of their own strength. Suffering abuse at the hands of another human being is also linked to a loss of trust in people and the world around them.

By helping the abuse victim to understand the body language of others, they can be aided in evaluating the world and those around them in terms of what they see, not what they fear. This is in itself already great empowerment to the abuse victim, as they can become a participant in life again, and feel like they have the power to make informed decisions.

Self-development

Being an effective communicator is one of life's great skills that will open doors and lead to the emboldening of the self. Self-development programs often include modalities on body language where the participants are trained in the uses of positive body language and assertiveness.

Group dynamics

People can be classed as two groups: introverts and extroverts. Introverts, as we know, are those people who tend to thrive in one-on-one communications and prefer to spend more time alone; while extroverts are the life of the party and go through life with a the-more-the-merrier attitude. Introverts often suffer a form of depression based on social settings. They do not do well in groups. As a result, their communication within a group dynamic tends to fizzle. Yet, communication is a learned skill. Like we learn the words, sentence structures, and grammar of a new language, we can also learn the way in which body language works.

Depression

People suffering from depression tend to convince themselves that they are not worthy, that they are to blame for some usually imaginary flaw, and that they are being judged by everyone around them. In the worst cases, this can lead to extreme paranoia.

People with depression sometimes think that everyone else has it good, while they alone are suffering. In creating awareness of body language, they can begin to see the world in a more realistic sense and realize that people everywhere go through trying times and that they are not alone.

By learning to focus on using positive body language they can also begin to manage their condition, as this will encourage feelings of well-being.

OCD

This condition is known for the repetitive behavior that someone engages in to make themselves feel in control of their lives. At the root of this tragic condition lies the fear of a loss of power and a profound distrust in themselves and in others. In extreme cases, this can even extend to excessive washing of hands to remove imaginary germs and then avoiding people because people have germs.

People with OCD tend to have a very negative view of the world, and their only safety comes from their repetitive behaviors. Using body language, they can be trained to notice positive feelings in others and to begin incorporating that into themselves. As they learn to project a positive self-image, they will feel their stress levels diminish, which will lead to a reduction of their anxiety-driven obsessions. When they feel more balanced, they will begin to develop trust in themselves and those around them.

Destructive body imagery (bulimia and obesity)

Poor body image is a tragic and very destructive condition to suffer from. It goes with low self-esteem, lack of trust, feelings of abandonment, and severe depression. Bulimia leads the sufferer to obsessively lose weight, while obesity is a condition where the sufferer wants to fill themselves due to their own emotional disabilities.

Both these conditions are associated with a loss of reality. These people begin to see the world not as it is, but as they believe it to be, and their world view is almost always negative. They eat, or refuse to eat, to hide from the world and themselves.

Body language is a way to find a connection back to the real world. In reading the body language being projected by those around us, we can begin to see that there are loads of people who are just like us. We are not alone. Using positive body language is one of the therapeutic ways to recover a sense of self that is realistic and beneficial.

The biological feedback mechanism of body language

Due to our loss of trust in other humans, we often turn to animals for comfort and assurance. We read into what people do, what they say, how they say it, and how they react to us. A salesman will do this on a second-by-second basis where they monitor the body language of the client and adjust their body language to match. Techniques such as mirroring, open position, advancing or retreating, and touching can be used to have an effect on the other person, and monitor how persuasive we are being on them. If they have begun to trust us enough, they will begin to do something we want; in which case, we will trust them since they've done something for us. This endless, nonverbal loop is known as a biological feedback mechanism.

Training and exercises

There are numerous academies and colleges that strive to train people in body language detection and application. They mention facts and case-studies, what to do and what not to do; however, not many of them detail exactly how to improve your body language in a step-by-step way. When considering the activities and desired results, we suggest the following steps be followed:

Observe

Look at the world around you. Notice the people in it and how they interact with each other. Identify people in similar situations to those that challenge you. This could be someone applying for a promotion at work, asking a girl on a date, and even haggling for a discount. Each situation will use the same skills but in different ways. It all boils down to body language.

Take notes if you like, or snapshot the interactions to review later. This may seem like stalking behavior to some, but it is called vicarious learning in psychological circles. You learn from the behavior, whether successful or not, of others.

Practice

This will require some bravery, which is perhaps why people do crazy things in foreign lands where no one knows them. Find some friends, or set up a hidden camera if you have to, or go to obedience training with your dog. The goal is to place yourself in a situation where you can practice some of the skills and how they can be used.

If you feel overwhelmed, you can practice at home with a mirror. You might even find some online help with an online counselor who can perhaps observe you over Skype.

Evaluate

Look at the recording you made of yourself, or talk to friends who are helping you. Don't look at your awkwardness; rather, focus on each body language technique, how you applied it, and what the response to it was.

You may even give yourself a score or write down what you need to focus on. Remember to celebrate the successes, no matter how small. Then it's time to repeat step two, practice.

It may seem like an incredibly arduous task to learn body language, but it certainly is worth it. These skills of using space, posture, facial expressions, eye contact, gesture, and touch are vital to leading a fulfilling life that has less conflict and misunderstanding in it.

Chapter 16 Behavior, Deviant Behavior and Psychology

Behavioral psychology is a field of knowledge that explains the nonverbal movements of the body (facial expression, gestures, intonations) of a person and draws conclusions about how sincere, true, confident and open.

Very often we make such an assessment unconsciously when we feel uncomfortable when we are communicating with, or even avoiding, a familiar person. But we actually appreciate his behavioral manifestations, which tell us what he thinks of us, how he relates, despite the fact that his words may be sympathetic or neutral.

There are a number of techniques for determining a person's true intentions, his emotions, and his level of self-esteem. His movements, facial expressions, and other features reveal his inner fears, attitudes, complexes that we perceive unknowingly or consciously if we have some knowledge and experience.

We perceive the process of communication as a general picture, sometimes during a conversation, we do not notice what we are wearing, what it says, but we pay attention to how it does it, what phrases and words it uses, how it sits and what it holds in our hands. Sometimes the little thing gets attention and is remembered for a long time: smell, speech difficulty, accent, reservations, wrong accents, inappropriate giggles, etc.

The scientific discipline that helps to explain and decipher the unconscious nuances in the behavior of people who give their true intentions is the psychology of behavior.

1. What do gestures and facial expressions tell us?

Facial gestures and expressions play a huge role in the conversation. But despite the simplicity of decoding a person's postures and gestures, they can have a completely different meaning.

For example, in the psychology of lies, there are basic signs of deception: one does not look into his eyes, touch the mouth, nose, neck. But the other person can only touch his nose because of itching.

Crossed legs or arms - these gestures in the psychology of human behavior are interpreted as distrust, tightness, isolation, but the interlocutor may just be cold.

Tips for deciphering manners and gestures can often lead to a dead-end or confuse a person. For example, after seeing the interviewee's open position, confident and calm voice, the pleasant honest look, we consider him an honest man and in fact, he has deceptive intentions. Or pickups, how much charm, wit, sincerity, good breeding they have - and that's all they need to establish themselves.

2.   What do speech and intonation tell us?

Speech speed, rhythm, volume, intonation greatly influence communication and can tell a great deal more information about a person, as behavior psychology considers. Science helps to understand a person's emotional state:

• A calm, sensible, balanced person speaks rhythmically, slowly, with a moderate level of loudness.

• The impulsive character gives a quick and lively speech.

• Those who are not confident or closed-minded speak softly, hesitantly.

3. Often words are not as important as intonation.

But it must be understood that if a person is in an unfamiliar environment, he may behave differently than in a familiar environment.

The psychology of behavior will allow you to identify the hidden factors that actually affect a person. But in order to see and understand them, we need to be "grounded" through knowledge and attentive to people.

Deviant Behavior and Psychology

The phenomenon of such behavior is so complex and widespread that, in order to study it, there is a separate science - deviant theory, which emerged at the intersection of criminology, sociology, psychology, and psychiatry.

1. The concept of "deviant" and social behavior in psychology

"Deviation" from Latin - "Deviation" In psychology, deviant behavior from accepted norms in society is called deviant or asocial. It is a sustainable human behavior that causes real harm to people and society. This is harmful to others as well as to the deviant itself.

The psychology of deviant behavior explores such forms of deviation as suicide, crime, prostitution, drug addiction, wandering, fanaticism, alcoholism, vandalism.

Such behavior is related to anger, violence, aggression, destruction, therefore the society has conditionally or lawfully imposed penalties on the offender of social norms; it is isolated, treated, corrected or punished.

2. The identity of the deviant, his psychology, behavior

Science does not study how and where a person has committed a crime; she is interested in common patterns and personality traits.

Causes and sources of asocial behavior:

• Physiological: genetic predisposition to aggression; endocrine diseases; chromosomal abnormalities.

• Public: imperfect legislation; social inequality; promoting anti-social lifestyle in the media; hangs "labels"; negative evaluations they give to local people.

• Psychological causes: internal conflicts between conscience and desires; special character of the character; mental anomalies; dysfunctional family relationships; too conservative, rigorous, cruel upbringing in childhood.

In the nature of deviations, characteristics such as conflict, negativism, dependence, anxiety, aggression, hostility are common. They often cheat and do it with pleasure, they like to transfer responsibility and blame to others.

A person's deviant behavior leads to social maladaptation, i.e. does not adapt to the conditions of society and, as a result, opposes it.

The child's behavior cannot be asocial as children under the age of 5 have not yet developed self-control and the process of adaptation in society has just begun.

The most dangerous period in terms of the possibility of deviation between the ages of 12 and 20 years.

3. How to deal with behavior problems?

Most often people with such behavior go to a psychologist already in detention centers, in children's colonies, in addiction treatment centers. The society deals with the prevention of deviations in hospitals, schools, the media, but the problem is that there is no individual approach and one cannot handle it alone. But he may realize the need to change his lifestyle and seek the help of specialists.

Psychology of Addictive Behavior

In psychology, addiction is called the science of human behavior, attachment to someone or something. It is unacceptable from the point of view of moral or social norms, endangering the health and causing suffering to the person.

Addiction harms society and humans, limits its development and leads to all kinds of mental illness.

More people die from addiction than crime and war together. It manifests itself as an escape from problems in an illusory ideal world. Gradually the person ceases to control his behavior, emotions, and thoughts. Its entire existence is reduced to the object of dependence, which gradually completely destroys it as a human being.

The widespread use of drugs and alcohol among young people has recently become a national disaster. That is why the attention of psychologists, psychiatrists, sociologists, drug addicts, and lawyers is directed at this issue.

Addictive behavior is also called addiction-this is a kind of deviant behavior. That is, the desire to escape from reality by changing your mental consciousness. Behavioral psychology sees this as a destructive attitude towards itself and society.

Addictive behavior includes alcoholism, drug addiction, smoking, increased libido, gambling, computer addiction, abundant food poisoning, and shopping.

Addiction has different weights, from normal to severe.

Why do some people form this strong and attractive attachment that explains the impulsiveness and frustration of attraction? The answers to these questions are most important for society and all individuals.

Psychology of Gestures and Facial Expressions

The psychology of behavior, gestures and facial expressions are the keys to the secrets of the person he wants to hide. As a result of evolution, man has learned to convey thoughts and feelings through words. But with this skill, he has mastered the art of hiding his true intentions and intentions, aspirations. You should be able to "read" your interlocutor in his gestures. Only in this way can one understand what is in his mind and what can be expected from him.

American psychologist Meyerabian Albert believes that when we communicate, we transmit 7% of the information verbally, 38% in intonation and tone of voice, 55% in non-verbal signals.

The basic rule of the psychology of gestures and facial expression is that there is no person in the world who can fully control the body's movements in the process of conversation, even if it wants to deliberately mislead the interlocutor.

A person at the subconscious level responds almost equally to certain situations. Forced facial expressions and gestures of a stranger allow you to hear and see the words hidden behind the screen.

• Protection. In dangerous or uncomfortable situations, when one wants to isolate himself from the other party - people lean back, close with a book, folder or another object, cross their legs, cross their arms over their breasts, clench their fists. Their eyes are closely watched by those who expect the trick. Such behavior is alert and tense and does not require constructive dialogue.

- Openness. The body is inclined towards the interlocutor, open palms, benign smile - these signals indicate a predisposition to communication.

- Interest. Lack of gestures, talking about enthusiasm, a person full of attention, he leans forward and tries not to move so he doesn't miss a word.

- Boredom. Gone is the sight, the rhythmic shaking of his feet, something in his hands, attraction, yawning. In sign language in the psychology of communication, this means that the listener has no interest in the topic of the conversation.

- Skeptical. The man agrees with the interlocutor but makes it clear that he does not trust such gestures as rubbing the neck, scratching his ear, cheek, forehead, smile, stuffing his chin with his palm.

The psychology of human behavior teaches us to understand the wisdom of non-verbal symbolism and the proper understanding of one another.

What Does Male Behavior Tell Us

The strong half of humanity's psychology is always about performing certain actions. Conquer, win, and conquer. Therefore, in their childhood games, there is always a spirit of endurance, character strength, strength competition

All actions are aimed at the final result. Their self-esteem since childhood is based on ability and achievement.

The words and actions of men and women are different. Therefore, when talking to them, you need to pay attention to the overall behavior. If he sits half turned with his legs and an arm crossed during a conversation and does not listen, he will somehow block the information. When he looks into his eyes and sometimes sees his lips, he is passionate about conversation.

When a man straightens his tie, he changes his posture, raises his eyebrows, opens his eyes-he is interested in the woman who is talking.

If he avoids searching, pulling buttons, or other small details of clothing, covering his mouth with his hand and not keeping his shirt collar straight, the interviewee is trying to hide something.

Note that all these non-verbal signals are average. Strong sex psychology is much more complex and depends on the person and his emotional fullness.

Psychology of Women

The psychology of the beautiful half of humanity is based on several circumstances:

•   The nature of the warehouse. Most women are optimistic. They are active, they are characterized by changes in mood, and they are able to control the feelings, subordinate circumstances of their desires.

•   Education - What parents put in a little girl determines her actions and behavior.

•   Experience - If she has been confronted with negativity throughout her life, she stops believing in people and becomes lonely. Her behavior is different from the standard.

The psychology of a woman's behavior is determined by her attitude towards the man. Psychologists believe that women have natural resourcefulness that helps them in their lives. But they focus their ingenuity on relationships with men. For example, they try to look strong and independent, always have hobbies and hobbies, often plan personal time and so on.

Chapter 17 Interpreting and Understanding Personality Type and their Main Characteristics

Given this reaction, what kind of personality do you think your boss had? Do you think he would have acted differently if he had a different personality? Yes, he probably would have. But why would a difference in personality have made a change in reaction?

An individual's 'personality' is loosely defined as a collection of traits and characteristics that give people their distinctive character. Throughout the years, there have been countless psychologists who have tried to encapsulate the meaning of a personality - from Freud, to Erikson, to Jung, and many others - and all of these experts have contributed greatly to our understanding of the abstract concept.

Knowing an individual's personality is an important part of decoding people because it tells you how they might act or speak. Their personality will show you their tendencies and social patterns, allowing you to generate a more accurate prediction of how a specific encounter might go.

The Myers Briggs Test

Carl Jung was a Swiss psychiatrist and psychoanalyst who dedicated most of his life to understanding the human psyche. Through his research, he was able to publish several books that gave readers his interpretations and understanding of the human personality. Soon, English translations of these books found their way into the hands of Katharine Cook Briggs - an academic and an avid reader and writer.

Prior to finding Jung's books, Briggs had already developed her own theories on personality. She formulated 4 categories of personality types after noticing that her soon-to-be son-in-law had a different set of characteristics compared to members of their family. Upon reading Jung's books however, she discovered that the psychoanalyst had a far more extensive understanding of personality.

This prompted her to further develop her system, which led to the iconic Myers-Briggs Type Indicator - a personality test that she developed with her daughter, Isabel Briggs Myers. This test is now used widely in employment and school evaluations.

Limitations of the Myers-Briggs Type Indicator

While it is widely used and applied in various fields of practice, the Myers-Briggs Type Indicator isn't without its flaws. In fact, throughout the years, countless critics have made comments about the MBTI's reliability, especially because it can give a person different results with each take.

On top of that, the test does not take neuroticism into account. So, individuals with neurotic tendencies might not be detected by the exam. Finally, the test doesn't provide any accurate measures for what it detects, so it's hard to understand exactly what it tries to understand given that the concept of personality is so abstract.

Even then, using the Myers-Briggs for purposes that include decoding a person can be good enough to get a better understanding of what lies underneath the surface. However, as any cautious detective, you need to be aware of the method's limitations to guide your premises and conclusions.

Attitudes

The first letter in every Myers-Briggs personality type refers to either extroversion or introversion so that each of the 16 types will either appear EXXX or IXXX. This first letter designates the individual's attitude, which was described by Myers as the tendency to act either inwardly or outwardly on thoughts and ideas.

Essentially, extroverts are more inclined to execute action. They move and speak to fuel their motivation. Without this physical manifestation of energy, their motivation has a tendency to decline. People who are introverts are more likely to reflect and think. They prefer inward manifestations of their energy and are more motivated with tasks that require rumination and deep thought.

Here are some of the basic differences of introverts and extroverts:

Extroverts	Introverts
Action oriented	Thought oriented
Prefer a wide knowledge base that crosses over to different concepts	Prefer a deep knowledge base that explains specific information in detail
Enjoy frequent interaction	Enjoy meaningful interaction
Draw energy from socialization	Draw energy from being alone

How do you identify an extrovert or introvert in public?

Of course, drawing this information back to Sherlock, the true value of knowing the attitude types is being able to detect them in real life situations. In this case, you might consider someone an extrovert if they seem to enjoy socializing, if they seem energized with physical activity, and if they present a commanding aura that takes control of interactions.

You might call someone an introvert if they prefer isolation, if they enjoy small meaningful gatherings and socialization, or if they seem energized when given the opportunity to explore ideas, thoughts, and concepts away from the company of other people.

During social interactions, it's possible that someone who is an extrovert might be more interested in direct engagement and conversation. They also tend to be far more vocal about their ideas and opinions, making them quite the challenge to debate with. On the other hand, someone who is an introvert might be much more comfortable having you take the reins of a conversation.

Introverts, as a general rule, are far harder to decode because they internalize everything they think and feel. However, because they are more interested in meaningful interaction, tapping into what they find important and relevant can make it possible for you to get them to become more expressive.

Functions

There are two pairs of functions according to Myers - these are the perceiving and the judging functions. The perceiving functions describe how a person interprets information or data, and the judging functions indicate a person's tendencies when it comes to making a decision based on the facts that have been presented.

The perceiving functions are sensation and intuition. As a general rule, people have dominant traits in a specific dichotomy, but it never means that the other is completely disabled. Everyone has these traits to some extent, it's just that one or the other is more prominent and likely to be used.

Sensation pertains to a method of information processing that uses the 5 senses. This is a more empirical method of data interpretation in which a person prefers to rely on details that are perceivable. They prefer to dwell on data that's present, tangible, and real as opposed to information that comes from hunches or guesswork.

Intuition on the other hand, is a method of information processing that dwells more on the unseen. These people use their gut to feel for the right conclusion, even if that means their conclusion won't be based on factual, tangible information. They're often more interested in the possibilities of the future, so they won't limit themselves to choices that are bound by facts.

The judging functions are thinking and feeling. These are decision making functions that are used when a person needs to arrive at a resolve given a set of information.

As the term suggests, people who use their thinking function to make a decision choose to do so from a somewhat detached standpoint. They use logic and reason and prefer to look at the facts before arriving at a thoroughly thought-out decision. However, that decision affects their emotions or the emotions of others around them isn't a top concern in the decision-making process.

On the other hand, people who use their feeling function when making a decision are more inclined to use the emotional context of the situation instead of simply dwelling on the facts. They prefer outcomes that generate harmony, making choices that suit the benefit and preference of the general census.

According to Jung, each person uses a dominant function in combination with an auxiliary function. The psychoanalyst has also suggested that we use a tertiary function to a much lesser extent, with the fourth function taking the role of a 'shadow'. In all cases, the shadow or fourth function is the opposite of the dominant function.

Lifestyle Preferences

In this dichotomy, there are two options - judging and perception. This is an added facet of the Myers-Briggs Type Indicator which wasn't available in Carl Jung's model. The purpose of this dichotomy is to decipher a person's preference in using either their judging or perceiving functions.

People who manifest the judging function as their lifestyle preference are those who navigate the world using their judging function most predominantly. This means that TJ individuals (or thinking/judging) are seen as logical people, while FJ individuals (or feeling/judging) are seen as empathetic.

In the same way, people who tend to prefer the perception navigate the world using one of the two perceiving functions. That said, individuals who are SP (sensation/perceiving) are seen as concrete individuals who use reliable facts. Those who are NP (intuitive/perceiving) are usually considered or labeled abstract thinkers.

The 16 Personality Types

Although Jung had originally come up with 32 personality types, the Myers-Briggs Type Indicator condensed the types into just 16. These personality types use combinations in each dichotomy to come up with a holistic idea of a person's tendencies.

While it doesn't specifically predict a person's reactions, it does tell you the kind of response you can expect.

The personality types shed light on the type of interaction a particular person might prefer, given the specifics they fall into under each dichotomy.

ISTJ	ISFJ	INFJ	INTJ
Sincere, analytical, reserved, realistic, hardworking, responsible, and trustworthy	Warm, considerate, gentle, thorough, pragmatic, devoted, caring, helpful, responsible	Idealistic, organized, compassionate, gentle, prefer harmony, enjoy intellectual stimulation	Original, innovative, independent, strategic, logical, reserved, insightful, driven
ISTP	ISFP	INFP	INTP
Action-oriented, enjoy understanding the mechanical functions of	Gentle, sensitive, flexible, helpful, realistic, interested in	Sensitive, creative, idealistic, caring, puts great value on inner harmony and	Logical, precise, reserved, flexible, original, enjoy speculation

things, spontaneous, analytical	practicality, strive for a personal space that's logical and beautiful	peace, focuses on dreams and goals	, can come up with creative solutions to problems, imaginative
ESTP Outgoing, realistic, action-oriented, curious, pragmatic, skilled negotiator	ESFP Playful, skilled at negotiating, strong common sense, friendly, spontaneous, tactful	ENFP Enthusiastic, creative, spontaneous, optimistic, supportive, enjoys engaging in new projects	ENTP Inventive, enthusiastic, versatile, inquisitive, strategic, enterprising, enjoys new and unfamiliar challenges
ESTJ Efficient, outgoing,	ESFJ Friendly, outgoing,	ENFJ Caring, enthusiastic,	ENTJ Strategic, logical,

analytical, realistic, systematic, dependable	reliable, practical, helpful, prefer to please others, enjoys activity and productivity	idealistic, organized, diplomatic, responsible, skilled communicators	efficient, outgoing, ambitious, long range planners, effective at organizing people

Understanding the personality types entails breaking its corresponding acronym down into parts. The first letter always represents the attitude which would either be extroverted or introverted.

The second and third letters are representative of the functions. As a general rule, this letter combination can't be represented by two letters from the same dichotomy. For instance, an individual can't be both sensing and intuitive since they're both perceiving functions. A person can't be both thinking and feeling since they're both judging functions. That said, the only combinations for the second and third letters can be SF, ST, NF, or NT.

Finally, the last letter in the 4-letter acronym represents the lifestyle preference for that specific personality. This can be either perceiving represented by P or judging represented by J.

All that considered, we can now decipher that a person who falls within the ISFJ personality type - the most common among the population - manifests an introvert-sensing-feeling-judging personality type.

Keep in mind that there's far more to each of these personality types than what's stated in this short table. In fact, each type comes with extensive elaborations that discuss the personality in depth, so it might be worth reading up on the different types to familiarize yourself with each one.

Stocking points of information for each type into your mind palace can help give you keys to understanding each person you encounter based on the type that you identify them to be.

Conclusion

Happy you have made it this far and I hope you found all the information stated here useful for day-to-day life. Explanations on body language and how it can help you decipher what people really think or feel situations. More importantly, we covered how you can use this information to communicate better with people.

Understand if things are a little bit confusing even at this stage—it's supposed to be. The fact is that understanding people is a lifetime process so you will find the need to constantly evaluate your baselines as you move forward.

Here's one thing I want you to remember: you only have control over your own values, actions, and reactions. It doesn't matter how badly you want to connect or forge ties with someone—you cannot make people like you if their values are intrinsically different from yourself. Keep in mind that connection is based on similarities and there's no point connecting with someone when nothing is similar between the two of you. Remember: you matter first. Your values are personal to you and you should NOT allow other people to predict your values.

So what do you do now? Here's what I want you to do:

Take a good look at yourself and assess your own values, personality, communication style, goals, and everything else that pertains to you. I want you to deeply get to know yourself first before attempting to know others.

Your next step would be to observe yourself. What are your mannerisms, your behavior, your tendencies when confronted with specific situations? I want you to know exactly what you're doing wrong and what you're doing right.

Next is cultivating a system of thinking, analyzing, and discovering your own values and motivations before pursuing a behavior. Even before you do something, I want you to pause and think about why you're doing it. What's your ultimate goal and what's the motivation behind it? Feel free to use Maslow's Hierarchy of Needs for this to help you further narrow down your own motivations.

Once you've figured out your goals and motivations, I want you to take a good look at the actions you propose to take. Are those actions in line with your goals and motivations? Will they achieve the results you want? What other roads are there for you to take in order to get the same results, but with much less hindrance on your part?

I encourage you to practice these four steps consistently in order to get to know yourself better and deeper through personal analysis. Only after you're comfortable understanding yourself can you feel comfortable in understanding others. One thing I want you to remember though: you don't have to understand yourself 100%! Face it, people are a mystery and sometimes, we can be a mystery to ourselves too. All I encourage you to do is to try as often and as hard as you can to trace your motivations before pursuing any sort of significant action.

So let's say you're comfortable understanding your own motivations at this point…what about other people? First, I discourage you against reading too much into people you don't know or barely know. While thin-slicing is highly effective, you should not use this as a way to figure out everything around you. People-watching can be fun and a good way to hone your skills, but don't take things too seriously.

Start by focusing only on a small group of people. Make decisions based on conscious "reading" efforts, but keep it simple or in situations where getting it wrong wouldn't have negative consequences in your life. Remember, you're testing the waters here and just honing your skills.

Always keep in mind that this book was written to help you CONNECT with people through developed verbal and non-verbal skills. Hence, try not to use your new superpowers for evil and keep connections in mind when trying to decipher people.

Have a pattern when observing people. This means having a fairly good idea of where to start when attempting to understand them. For example, you look at the feet first, then the hands, then face, or any other sequence you may choose. Having this pre-set programming on where to look gives you a story-type reading experience that can help with any conclusions you might have about the situation. The beauty here is that as you practice this technique, it becomes second nature to the point where you don't even have to consciously guide yourself through the process. Your mind instantly goes to these body parts in order to interpret what they mean.

Learn the art of listening and try not to be too self-absorbed. Even as an extrovert, you should be able to recognize the enjoyment of being able to sit back in one corner of the room and just take in the different movements and reactions of people as they interact with each other.

If you find things too difficult, I suggest you watch a movie multiple times and pay attention not just to the words but also to the actions and movements of the actors. Actors are trained in the proper action and reaction in different situations. Their facial expressions and even the slightest movement of the hands can convey so much and can help hone your skills in prediction. It's by far the safest way of approaching body language understanding while enjoying yourself in the process. Make sure to watch movies with very good actors known for their excellent skills in the art. Meryl Streep movies are perhaps one of the best to do this, focusing primarily on the movement of this amazing actress.

The beauty of watching movies is that there's a way for you to confirm what you suspect about a certain situation. You can look at a person's expression in one scene and guess on what they think or feel. In a later scene, these emotions are often expressed out loud or given further focus, therefore allowing you to really figure out if what you initially thought was correct.

When reading people in the real world, observe and keep your conclusions to yourself. Do not go around telling people that you've "read" how a particular coworker acts and make expressive predictions because of it. I want you to keep any conclusions or ideas you have close to your heart and only use them when needed.

Practice, practice, practice! The beauty of reading body language is that you never run out of people to observe or body language to read. There's always an endless supply of them, so feel free to practice as often as you want. Note though that acting on those observations isn't always advisable. Think about it multiple times before actually making a decision.

Yes—you can read people and making connections simply by honing your verbal and non-verbal skills! But it takes time, patience, and drive. It might seem like such a big project at first, but don't let this stop you! Unless you live under a rock, forging connections and communicating with others is an integral part of your life. You will find that by mastering this talent, you too can achieve a kind of success that only few can boast about.